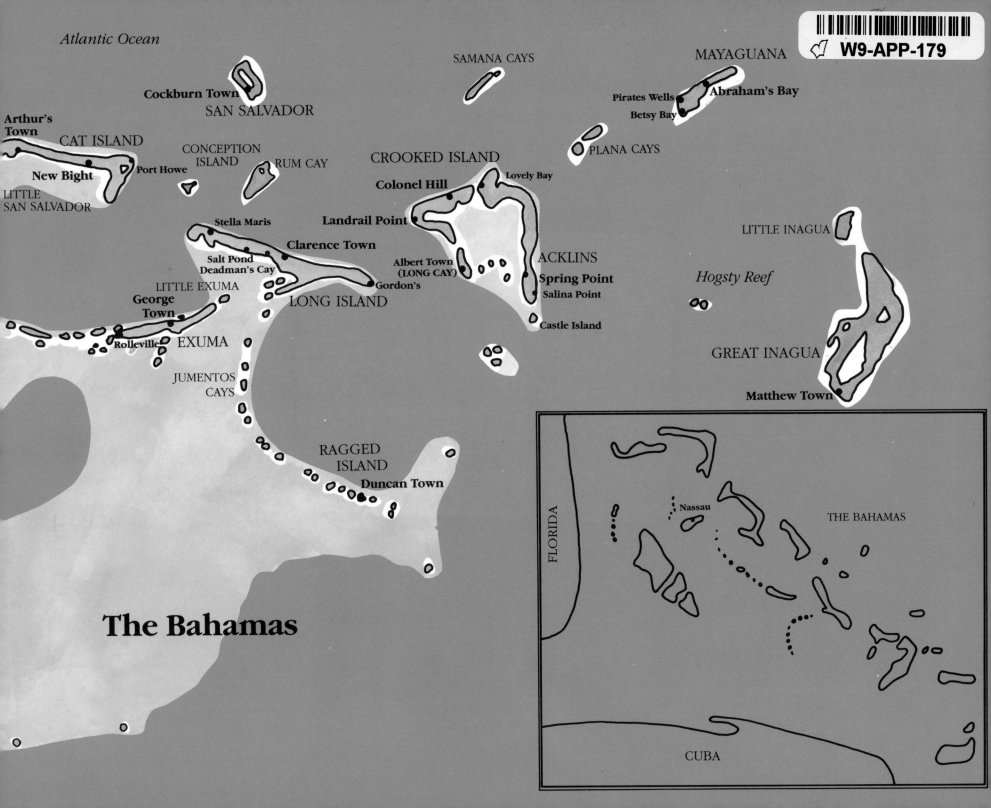

**Doral Golf Resort & Spa
And Nordic Empress Cruise
October 10-14, 1996**

THE BAHAMAS REDISCOVERED

NICOLAS AND DRAGAN POPOV

First published 1992

PUBLISHED BY THE MACMILLAN PRESS LTD
London and Basingstoke
*Associated companies and representatives in Accra, Auckland, Dehli, Dublin,
Gaborone, Hamburg, Harare, Hong Kong, Kuala Lumpur, Lagos, Manzini,
Melbourne, Mexico City, Nairobi, New York, Singapore, Tokyo.*

ISBN 0-333-56603-3

Printed in Hong Kong

A catalogue record for this book is available from the British Library.

(TITLE PAGE) AT THE SOUTHERN END OF LONG
ISLAND, THE SANDS NEAR THE SETTLEMENT OF
GORDON'S ARE ENJOYED BY LOCAL CHILDREN.
FEW OUTSIDERS KNOW THIS PLEASURE.

Dedication

To the memory of our father,
Dr Ivan M. Popov

Acknowledgements

We wish to thank Jane Sydenham Popov for the story on Columbus and the native Indians. Jane drew the map and with Linda D'Aguilar was very helpful in proofreading the manuscript. Also we would like to acknowledge Dave Baker for his assistance in the Nassau section and Pat Rahming for his poem. *The Bahamas Rediscovered* was realised from part of an extensive documentary exploration to all the islands over a period of six years. Support to the research expeditions was kindly made by various individuals and companies who deserve further acknowledgement. Foremost, to Vincent Coleby and Pauline Petty of Shell Bahamas Ltd, to Philip Smith of the Quincentennial Commission, to Portia Jordan and Neil Sealey of the College of The Bahamas, to Brendon Lynch of Euro-Dutch Trust, to Gail Saunders of the Archives, to Colin Higgs of the Department of Fisheries, to the Ministry of Tourism, and to any other individuals' support, we extent our sincere appreciation. We are especially grateful to Paul L. Knowles who contributed much of his time to the project, to students and children participating in the expeditions and most of all to the islanders' warm and friendly hospitality which can never be forgotten. Finally to our mother, Brigitte, whose encouragement has made this book possible.

Photo credits

All photography by the authors except for page 16 Eric Popp Island Expedition; page 36 (top) Jonathan Rimmen Island Expedition; page 51 (top) courtesy The Lucayan Beach Resort and Casino; page 113 (left) Philip Dutton Island Expedition.

(OPPOSITE) ONE OF THE MANY JEWELS IN THE CHAIN OF THE EXUMA CAYS.
(ABOVE) A GRANDMOTHER AND HER GRANDSON ON ABACO.

Introduction

A visitor peering for the first time at The Bahamas through an aeroplane window will immediately be struck by the many colours in the sea. The myriad shades of blue, green and turquoise water swirling amongst a string of islands and glittering sand banks can only make him or her want to plunge into the warm transparent sea. It is no wonder that The Bahamas attracts many visitors each year.

The Bahamas derives its name from the water surrounding the islands. It was named 'Bahamar', meaning 'shallow seas' by Christopher Columbus. The name was later changed to 'The Bahamas'. Stretching six hundred miles from Inagua in the south to Walkers Cay in the north, and nearly as far along the Tropic of Cancer from San Salvador in the east to Cay Sal in the west, The Bahamas is the largest of all island chains in the Caribbean. Its seven hundred islands, with their numerous rocks and small cays, are surrounded by large banks. These fringes of shallow water, where the depth ranges from a few inches off the coral reefs to an average of 50 feet on the furthest edges, mark the frontiers of The Bahamas; a unique archipelago, where the islands are merely the exposed tops of a massive limestone platform, blessed with the clearest water in the world.

The sea is the pivot on which life has always hinged in The Bahamas. For Bahamians who used to salvage valuable goods from boats wrecked on the coral reef, for fishermen who continue to collect fish, conch and lobster, and especially for today's booming tourism industry, the sea has always been the provider.

The Bahamian islands have their own character and ambience which have developed from their geographical isolation and the number of immigrants from Africa, America and Europe. Descended mostly from African forebears, the people act and see themselves as Bahamians in a society in many ways different from its distant continents of origin, one that is changing day by day. Over half of the population of 250,000 lives on the main island of New Providence where the glamorous capital of Nassau sits overlooking the harbour and adjacent Paradise Island. The remainder of the population is spread in small and large communities in all the other islands. Places like Marsh Harbour in Abaco, George Town in Exuma, Alice Town in Bimini, Rock Sound in Eleuthera, Spanish Wells and Harbour Island are the largest of over two hundred other communities found in these serene and peaceful islands once called the 'Out Islands'.

While Nassau and Freeport are at the commercial heartbeat of The Bahamas, providing its people with an economic and political structure, most of its inherent customs, traditions and ways of life are found in the other islands. While these islands were once considered outer islands, they have a strong and unshakeable connection with the main centres, not only because of the large migration of their people to Nassau and Freeport but because they have the natural resources, friendly people and the most unspoiled environment of The Bahamas. For these reasons, these islands, previously considered as being removed from the jetstream of industry have, since the 1980s, adopted the appropriate name of the 'Family Islands'.

At one time the people of the islands were completely dependent upon the available resources and the knowledge they held in common on how to survive in their immediate environment. There are still people on the more remote islands who forge, salvage, fish, collect rain water, farm in pot holes, build rock and limestone houses, cook over wood fires, and make medicinal teas from local plants. The many images in this book represent a rich culture and lifestyle that is changing rapidly. One common scene may be children fishing on the dock of their island settlement or happily sculling their father's home-made wooden boat. Picking seagrapes or dillies on the way home, the children will bring the catch of the day to be cooked on an open fire and shared with tales of yesterday. It is easy to wonder how many more of the Family Islands' youth will move to Nassau and Freeport.

Mainly because of the migration to the capital, the Bahamian people have acquired two different types of life.

You are either a 'city boy' or an 'island boy' and few manage to be both. The choice is between living in Nassau or Freeport or living in the Family Islands. Many more have chosen the former.

Since Nassau became the governmental headquarters of The Bahamas, with its convenient deep water harbour for importation of goods (then coming mostly from the Family Islands), the population has steadily grown. Later, increased tourism, the newly developed city of Freeport and the independence of 1973 attracted more and more people from the Family Islands who found a variety of jobs. Both urban metropolises expanded tremendously, and naturally, the way of life changed drastically. Dependency on available resources diminished as the large towns imported, for the most part, all goods necessary to live in a modern society. Today's city boy lives on one bustling island which has a larger population than all the other islands put together, with a couple of million tourists visiting each year and an immigrant Haitian population seeking a better life.

Surrounded by the seemingly endless miles of shallow-water banks, Nassau, Freeport and the Family Islands all make up The Bahamas. *The Bahamas Rediscovered* attempts to view the whole country: to present its history from the time Columbus stepped on its shores five hundred years ago and to rediscover the unique features of each one of its islands, not forgetting one because it seems too far away and seldom trodden.

STANIEL CAY, EXUMAS.

When I claim my name
I claim my share in a life
of the discovery of the treasures of nature
and of the enjoyment of my wealth:
the gold of sunshine,
turquoise of the sea
the silver of the soil
and the bronze and ebony of my people
I claim the right
to know my country
well enough to feel its heart
pound inside my chest
and its blood racing through my veins,
to cry when it is grieved by some act of insensitivity
and to laugh at its youthful naivety.

> For strangers see my land
> Isles of palm trees in the sand
> A place to buy
> A place for fun
> A place that pleases everyone
> But this is my home
> and I claim the name
> Bahamian

from the poem
I AM A BAHAMIAN
by Pat Rahming

A HORSE AND SURREY ALLOW VISITORS TO TOUR THE CITY OF NASSAU IN STYLE.

(OPPOSITE) A TYPICAL STOP-OFF IN THE FAMILY ISLANDS.

A GOOD DAY'S CATCH. THE CRAWFISH INDUSTRY IS OF MAJOR IMPORTANCE TO
THE BAHAMIAN ECONOMY.

JUNKANOO – A COLOURFUL DISPLAY OF BAHAMIAN CULTURE.

THE TRADITIONAL FAMILY ISLAND REGATTA.

ELEGANT
WEST INDIAN
FLAMINGOS
ARE FOUND IN
THE REMOTEST
PARTS OF THE
BAHAMAS.

(OPPOSITE)
FISH OF EVERY
IMAGINABLE COLOUR
AND SIZE IN THE
THOUSANDS OF
CORAL REEFS OF THE
BAHAMIAN
ARCHIPELAGO.

The Lucayans and the arrival of Columbus

It was morning and some of the men were already at work along the shoreline preparing for the day's fishing expedition. A young girl played at the water's edge, while her mother and the other women prepared cassava bread in the nearby settlement.

Suddenly a cry went up from one of the men. On the horizon there loomed an astonishing sight; three strange objects were gradually taking shape as they neared the coast. The white wings of the gigantic monsters collapsed as they glided to a halt and people could be seen clambering off them into small, broad craft. Were the visitors friend or foe, or even of this world? Panic mingled with curiosity. Should the onlookers run and hide, as from the barbaric southern tribes, or should they bow down in reverence to the strangers?

We can only guess at how the natives of Guanahani felt on the morning of October 12th, 1492, as they greeted the entourage from Europe; the overdressed, bearded demi-gods with their elaborate head wear and shining sticks, which cut the hands of the curious inhabitants as they grabbed them.

The people Columbus encountered some five hundred years ago called themselves 'lukka kairi', or men of the islands, and they are known to us today as the Lucayan Indians. Columbus was obviously impressed by their gentle nature when he described them as being 'so full of love and without greed ... that I believe there is no better race'. The strong, slender men and women, adorned with little more than coloured paints and perhaps a cotton mantle about their waists, had thick dark hair and impressive, wide foreheads. Their unwritten language was lyrical and soft.

The ancestry of these people is by no means certain, but there is strong evidence that they had been in The Bahamas for some seven hundred years before the arrival of the three caravels. They spoke a language derived from Arawak and had strong links with the Tainos of Hispaniola (today's Haiti and Dominican Republic) who, in turn, originated from the mainland of South America.

The Lucayans lived in small villages of perhaps a dozen dwellings built from wood and leaves and thatched with palm fronds. They were an agricultural society, relying on crops such as corn, sweet potato and cassava, which they made into a type of bread. The plentiful seas provided conch and fish, and their diet was enriched by the meat of the iguana and hutia – a rabbit-sized rodent.

Since they had no metal, the Lucayan tools were simple. Large trees, felled using strategically placed hot coals, were carved into canoes by burning out the centre with hot embers and chipping them into shape with the sharp edges of conch shells. Utensils were moulded out of clay, reinforced during the firing process by an outer layer of leaves or palms. They grew cotton, weaving it into cloth, fishing nets and 'hamaca', known to us as hammocks.

The indigenous people of The Bahamas lived a hard but peaceful life. However, it is thought that their tranquillity was sometimes destroyed by the invasion of fearsome cannibalistic tribes from the south. These Caribs carried away the islanders, who did not possess the weapons or the mentality to fight back. Columbus observed that some of them bore scars which they explained were the result of such attacks.

What of the newcomers who appeared in the bay that October morning? Ask any Bahamian school child and he or she will tell you that Columbus sailed across the ocean

SAN SALVADOR, THE SITE OF COLUMBUS' FIRST LANDING IN THE BAHAMAS

in 1492 and discovered America, but the first place he landed was The Bahamas. They will also reel off the names of his ships, the *Pinta, Niña* and the *Santa Maria*.

The name we use for the renowned 'Admiral of the Ocean Seas', as he would like to be remembered, is Christopher Columbus, an anglicised form of the Italian Cristoforo Colombo. Born in 1451, Christopher was the eldest son of a Genoese wool weaver. He made the acquaintance of the sea at a young age. Genoa, in Italy, was a busy port and, in the employment of his father, the young Columbus made numerous sea journeys aboard merchant ships.

The year 1481 found Columbus in the service of King John of Portugal. A trade route had already been set up with the rich Gold Coast of Africa and Columbus was in command of a caravel in a fleet bound for this area, helping establish a fort at Elmina. It was claimed that a trade route to the exotic treasures of the Orient could be made by rounding the African continent, and various expeditions were pushing further and further south to find the route. On his return from Africa, Columbus proposed to King John that an alternative route was feasible, travelling west across the Atlantic Ocean, known for its unforgiving tempests and enormous sea monsters, amongst other evils. Beyond it, Columbus was sure he would find Japan and China.

The king and a board of advisors rejected Columbus' proposals, but went ahead and financed other abortive attempts, leaving Columbus to spend almost nine years travelling back and forth between European royal courts in search of a serious financial sponsor.

At last, in April 1492, a proposal was drawn up; Columbus was to head three boats on a journey to the west in the name of King Ferdinand and Queen Isabella of Spain. On August 2nd of that year, the fleet left Palos in Spain. Columbus led the fleet in a three-masted ship of 100 tons – the *Santa Maria*; the two smaller, shallow draft caravels were captained by the Pinzon brothers of Palos. Each boat held enough supplies for a year, with small cannon and firearms at hand in case of trouble. Columbus' plan was quite simple. He knew that Japan lay on the same latitude as the Canary Isles, so after stopping there to make alterations to the *Niña*'s rig, he headed due west.

Leaving the Canaries on September 6th, the tiny fleet of ships first encountered unfavourable winds, but soon luck changed and a steady westerly breeze and tranquil seas allowed them to cover a thousand miles in just one week. The going was so good that many of the crew doubted their chances of return. Fearing they had embarked on what they thought was a one way journey into the unknown, they became tense. On September 20th, the tradewinds died and a change of direction was made. Soon the fleet was almost becalmed. One can imagine the relief when, on 25th September, the *Pinta*'s captain gave the jubilant cry of '*Tierra*!', quickly verified by the other lookouts. Everyone celebrated, gave thanks to God and changed course for the land to the south-west, only to be disappointed. Morale was low. A similar disappointment twelve days later was too much to bear. By October 10th, Columbus agreed to an ultimatum from his desperate crew: if land was not sighted within three days, they would turn back.

The next day, luck, or perhaps good judgement seemed to be on Columbus' side. Twigs and foliage were sighted floating in the water, birds flew overhead and, by late evening, the call of '*Tierra*!' went up from a seaman aboard the *Pinta*. This time there were no disappointments. The next morning, Columbus and his men rowed

CARLTON CARTWRIGHT (PICTURED) DISCOVERED IMPORTANT LUCAYAN CEREMONIAL STOOLS, KNOWN
AS 'DUHOS', INSIDE THIS CAVE IN SOUTHERN LONG ISLAND.

ashore on the western side of a low lying island, planted the Royal Standard of Ferdinand and Isabella and gave thanks to God for their safe arrival in this new land. Columbus named the island San Salvador and claimed it for his sovereigns.

The bewildered natives, reassured by the white men's gifts of glass beads and caps, were soon swimming out to the boats with gifts of their own such as parrots, balls of cotton and spears. Columbus and his expedition spent two days exploring the island the natives called Guanahani. Some of the Lucayans wore small gold ornaments and indicated that, if Columbus sailed south, he would find a country rich in this metal. Their directions confirmed what Columbus believed; he had reached the northern islands of Japan, where the emperor lived in a palace roofed with gold.

After two days of exploration, the party was ready to leave, taking with them seven natives as guides. The second island was reached by October 15th and named Santa Maria de la Conception, probably today's Rum Cay. Here too, the islanders confirmed that gold could be found to the south. For the next two weeks Columbus explored The Bahamas, his diary becoming ever more poetic as he saw more of the archipelago, describing the islands as 'the best, the most fertile, temperate and beautiful'.

As to his exact path through The Bahamas, there is much debate. The descriptions given by Columbus have been interpreted in many different ways and The Bahama islands, with their low coastlines and superficially similar terrains, have not made things easy for historians. The generally accepted view is that the expedition went on from Rum Cay to Long Island, which he called Fernandina, east to the tip of Crooked Island (Isabella),

and then south-west to the Ragged Islands (Isla de Arena). Columbus, by his estimations, was heading for the islands of Japan when he left The Bahamas on October 27th. He reached the shores of the large island the natives called Colba (Cuba) the next day, continuing the fervent search for gold.

The people of The Bahamas had charmed Columbus with their subservient hospitality. He wrote, 'they ought to be good servants and of good skill, for I see that they repeat very quickly all that is said to them'. This comment was to be of significance later, but for now, Columbus had no more interest in The Bahamas. There was no gold and therefore nothing worth staying for.

On this his first trip, Columbus was determined to forge good relations with the people he encountered. He did take a few of the inhabitants back to Spain under sufferance, but also managed to gain the confidence of many of the indigenous people and, most importantly, the friendship of Guacanagari, an important chief on Hispaniola. Leaving a garrison of men on lands ruled by the chief, Columbus returned to Spain to report to his sovereign. In his three subsequent voyages across the Atlantic Columbus never again set eyes on the graceful Lucayans, yet his observations had already sealed their fate.

On his return, the rapport that had been such an asset to his endeavours had collapsed. The Spaniards at the garrison abused the good will of the natives, setting a trend which rapidly became worse. Soon the entire population of Hispaniola was in servitude; the quest for gold was out of control and blinded any form of compassion. As the Tainos died under the strain of meeting impossible demands, the Spanish slavers turned to The Bahamas for their work force. Virtually the whole population was transplanted to mine the scant gold of Hispaniola and by 1530 The Bahamas had been depopulated.

The only notable exploration of The Bahamas at this time was carried out by Ponce de Léon. A member of Columbus' second voyage, he set off from Puerto Rico in 1513 with three ships in search of the fabled 'Fountain of Youth' on the island of Bimini. His quest took him the full length of The Bahama Islands from south to north.

The next century of Bahamian history is a blank page; the archipelago was left in silence, occasionally visited by ships to replenish water supplies. However, the dangerous reefs and banks of The Bahamas were generally considered a place to avoid.

It was not until 1648 that potential conquerors of a different kind walked on the shores of The Bahamas. Their conquest was not man against man, but rather man against nature. They initially lost their battle but, in time, learned to work with the land and sea as the Lucayans had done before them.

AN EIGHTEENTH CENTURY BREAD OR 'DUTCH' OVEN. THIS METHOD OF BAKING IS STILL COMMON IN THE BAHAMAS.

Nassau, Paradise Island and History

The first attempt to create a permanent settlement in The Bahamas ended in failure. In 1648 William Sayle and a party of would-be colonists from Bermuda landed on the island they named Eleuthera. They hoped to farm the islands but for the most part the ground was rocky and barren and their efforts were unsuccessful. This pioneering group were given the name 'Eleutheran Adventurers'.

The second attempt to organise a colony in The Bahamas was fundamentally different, and revolved around the sea and the wealth that it contained. The Bahamian way of life and its commercial success still looks to the sea.

William Sayle, on one of his many cruises to aid his colony, was forced to take refuge on an unknown island to avoid a storm. There he found a fine harbour nestled between the main island and a smaller island offshore. In gratitude for his salvation, he named the island 'Providence'. The fine harbour attracted more visiting ships but the name was changed to 'Sayle's Island' after its discoverer.

From 1666 the island became a haven for Bermudian sailors who used the harbour as a whaling base and somewhere from which they could look for wrecked Spanish ships. In 1670, a second group of Bermudian colonists decided to try to make The Bahamas their home.

This time they chose Sayle's Island which they called by its first name, 'Providence'. They called the town they founded next to the harbour 'Charles Town'. Within a few years, the prefix 'New' was added to the island's name to differentiate it from other Providences and, in 1695, the town was renamed Nassau after the Prince of Orange-Nassau, who had become William III, King of England.

Today, Nassau, on the 21-mile-long island of New Providence, is a bustling, vibrant city of 150,000 people. It is still, as it was at its founding and has been throughout its history, dependent upon the sea for its livelihood and commerce.

A quick walk through the streets of Nassau today reveals a varied and lively city. Colonial government buildings stand side-by-side with high-tech office buildings. International bankers in neat three-piece suits share the streets with tourists in plaid shorts, ordinary shopkeepers and Rastafarians in dreadlocks, wearing fatigues and Bob Marley T-shirts. Police in distinctive white uniforms guide the traffic at street corners from stands sheltered by umbrellas; women dress in colourful floral dresses to attend church on Sunday. The old and the new, history and the future, are woven into a remarkable tapestry that could only exist in The Bahamas.

Pirates

The inherent peacefulness of The Bahamas of today makes it hard to imagine the rowdy rough and tumble Nassau of the first years of the colony. Although originally settled by Puritans escaping from religious persecution on their home island of Bermuda, the colony was soon found to be advantageously placed for a very specific type of sea-going commerce – 'pirating'. New Providence Island is close to the three main routes out of the West Indies towards Europe, a fact that was quickly recognised by the pirates and privateers who preyed on the Spanish, French and English ships that used the routes. Within a few years, Nassau became the main base for some of the worst criminals ever to sail the seas. For the next fifty years, the town became the lawless base of the likes of Edward Teach (better known as Blackbeard), Jack Rackham, Stede Bonnet, Anne Bonny, Mary Read, and the champion of all pirates, 'Black Bart Roberts', a well-educated, former gentleman farmer who was reputed to have taken over 400 ships before he was killed.

There is little left in Nassau today to remind the visitor of that rowdy and bawdy past. The boisterous taverns that were open all night, the loud arguments over games of chance, the duels (like the one Mary Read fought to keep her lover from being killed), are all gone. Their memory is kept alive on *El Bucanero*, a replica of a seventeenth century pirate ship, which offers daytime and evening cruises around Nassau. The only other monument left from that era is a tower east of Nassau which is said to have been the watch tower used by Blackbeard to keep a lookout for those who would have his head.

Woodes Rogers

The pirating days of Nassau were soon notorious even in their own time and the proprietors, who owned the colony, sold it to the British Crown in the early years of the eighteenth century. The King sent Woodes Rogers to Nassau in 1718 as the first Royal Governor of the colony. His first task was to enforce law in the town and get rid of the pirates. Rogers knew enough about the bad reputation of the colony to take with him a small army, paid for out of his own pocket. When he reached Nassau he took the prudent step of sending one of his ships into the harbour first. When his ship drew fire from a pirate ship, Woodes Rogers landed his army, taking the colony by surprise. His first act as Governor was to offer the pirates amnesty. Those who refused to accept his offer were hunted down, often by reformed pirates, like Benjamin Hornigod. It was a hard struggle, but Woodes Rogers finally brought civilisation to Nassau.

Woodes Rogers himself had a history just as interesting as the more famous characters whom he evicted from Nassau. He was born in Bristol, the same town as Edward Teach. He was himself a 'privateer', which was a more legalised form of piracy whereby only ships that belonged to an enemy of your country were attacked, a line which was typically not very distinct and often completely obscured. Among Woodes Rogers' other prizes, he took what was undoubtedly the richest and most desirable prize of the era: the Spanish Black Ship of 1709. The black ships were a series of huge galleons that annually carried the treasures plundered from Mexico to Europe. He also was the captain who rescued the marooned 'Alexander Selkirk', soon to become famous as the model for the hero of Daniel Defoe's book, *Robinson*

Crusoe. This background in pirating helped Woodes Rogers live up to his motto, '*Expulsis Piratis–Restituta Commercia*' (he expelled pirates and restored commerce), a motto which has been adopted by The Bahamas.

Wreckers and Smugglers

Woodes Rogers did not, however stop the questionable activities of some Bahamians. From that day until the present, two of the major occupations in The Bahamas have been wrecking and smuggling. Wrecking is the act of salvaging goods and stores from the thousands of ships that have been wrecked on the many beautiful, yet deadly, coral reefs in The Bahamas. Thousands of ships, from Spanish galleons to modern cargo ships, have gone down in the treacherous waters. The wreckers saved thousands of lives and millions of dollars' worth of goods, many of them desperately needed by the small colony. Wreckers, however, did not always just happen upon a wreck. Most of the wrecking was probably quite legal, but there were times when even a wrecker's days were lean. Stories are told of wreckers lighting fires on the beach deliberately to drive an unsuspecting ship on to a convenient reef. There are even stories of deals made between a ship's captain and the wreckers to split the profits of a future venture devised by the captain himself. He would 'accidentally' run aground on to a reef convenient to the wrecker. It was not until better navigational aides, such as the Paradise Island lighthouse (which was built in 1817), and better charts were provided, that the islands of The Bahamas finally became safe for shipping.

When it comes to smuggling, Bahamians have always been very successful. Through the years, Bahamian smugglers have smuggled just about every imaginable item to just about any imaginable destination. Although The Bahamas has always been a colony of the British, Bahamians traded freely with enemies of the home country even during wars. The close and convenient proximity to the United States meant that The Bahamas was the port of choice to run the British blockades of the 1776-1783 revolutionary war, the Northern blockade of the Confederacy during the civil war of 1861-1865 and the government's blockade of the country during the years of prohibition (1920-1933). The practice continues today, as some small cays of The Bahamas are still used for drug smuggling.

The wreckers and the smugglers, while doing their part to keep the economy of the colony growing, have left little trace of their activities on the face of Nassau. The seas are safe for travellers and Nassau is an active, though not a rowdy city with a fine sense of the past.

The Loyalists

On a walk along Parliament Street through the public buildings and halls of government of the modern town, the visitor will be struck by the distinctive architecture. It is like being suddenly transported back to the great plantation era of the southern United States. When the British lost the American colonies (which were to become the United States), many loyalists either left the new country or were forced to leave by harassment. Between 1782 and 1783, some four to seven thousand of these loyalists found their way to The Bahamas, tripling the then population of the islands. Not only did this large influx of people create political problems between the former residents (who wanted things to remain the same as they had been) and the new arrivals (who wanted things to be the same as the place they had left, and to have a larger say in the running of the colony), it also brought a whole new culture to The Bahamas.

For the first and only time in the history of The Bahamas, the emphasis was not on the sea, but on the land. The loyalists, mostly plantation owners from Georgia and the Carolinas, brought their property (including slaves) and tried to raise cotton. The thin Bahamian soil was not suitable for that method of farming and, by the end of the century, the soil was exhausted and it was clear that the experiment had failed. The plantations that once nearly covered the island of New Providence are now gone, though at some, such as the Clifton plantation at the extreme western end, or the Love plantation which gave its name to nearby Love Beach, the crumbling ruins of the stately great houses and the walls that once secured the fields can still be seen.

Bahamians today

The plantation attempt was a failure but the influence of the southern states changed both the architectural style of the islands and the makeup of the Bahamian people. When the crops failed, the impoverished land owners moved on, leaving behind their former slaves, now freed, to become the forebears of the Bahamian people of today. Many of the smaller villages around New Providence Island towns, such as Gambier, Adelaide Village and Carmichael Village, were originally settled by the freed slaves from the nearby plantations.

The same government buildings that were built during the time of the loyalist influence are still in use for the daily operation of the government. It was from the upper storey of the House of Assembly that Lynden Pindling tossed the Speaker's Mace out of the window in April of 1965, a day that is remembered as 'Black Tuesday.' His words were, 'This Mace is the symbol of authority of this house and the authority belongs to the people and the people are outside.'

Pindling helped the blacks to a share of political power, the nation towards independence and himself to the role of first Prime Minister of the new nation. Next to the government buildings is Rawson Square where the statues of Queen Victoria, (symbolising the colonial period) and Milo Butler, (the first black governor, who symbolises independence), face each other on either side of Bay Street.

The heartbeat of Nassau has always been on Bay Street and it pounds hardest when the costumes, musicians and dancers of the Junkanoo parade rush down this main avenue. Following an African slave tradition, which celebrated music and dance after the hours of duty, the festival begins twice each year, in the dark morning hours of Boxing Day (26th December) and New Year's Day. It involves hundreds of people, organised in two major groups, the Saxons and Valley Boys, and an assortment of other smaller groups, each with their own theme. Prepared months in advance, the colourful floats are created out of papier mâché and are usually moved single-handedly to the rhythm of the music. Leading the large floats, the musicians keep the beat of drums, cowbells, whistles and horns going while dancers dart in and out of the scenery. 'Rushing' is the local term used when participating in Junkanoo and those who do not rush will watch behind the barricaded sidewalks or from a window, balcony, tree or roof of Bay Street. A few hours after sunrise the music stops, the winners are announced and all the costumes are put aside, never to be used again.

Historical Nassau

Another excellent example of the architecture of the loyalist period is Government House, the residence of the Governor General, who is the Queen's representative to the nation. Government House stands majestically above the city on the hill neatly dressed, just like all the other governmental buildings, in pink and white. The pink is known as 'Nassau pink' and is a symbol of two of the most distinctive natural features of the islands: the pink flamingo and the bright pink of the interior of the conch. The pink flamingo is undoubtedly one of the islands' most distinctive and beautiful birds, while the conch, which has a large and elegant shell, is one of the nation's favourite and most important food resources.

With the changes that time has brought to the city, it is surprising to see the number of buildings which still survive from the colonial age. Graycliff, which housed the West Indian Garrison that protected the city in the eighteenth and nineteenth centuries, is now one of the most elegant restaurants in Nassau. Jacaranda, with its wrap-around and enclosed verandas, is one of the best examples of the local style of architecture remaining. Lex House is one of the oldest buildings in the city and was used by the Spanish Governor from 1782 to 1783, the only period of time from its discovery until independence that the colony was not under British control. The city

Library is a fascinating octagonal building which was built in 1800 as the city jail then converted to a library in 1873. There is a dungeon in the basement and it also has a small museum. There is a panoramic view from the upper levels. All around the centre of the city are buildings that provide a glimpse of what Nassau of the colonial era must have looked like.

Some of the old Bahamian buildings have not endured. The large Royal Victoria Hotel, for example, which was once the place where confederate smugglers (including the man used as the character for Rhett Butler in *Gone With the Wind*), were watched by Union agents, and where the rich and famous rubbed elbows with rum runners during prohibition, is now in a complete state of disrepair.

The three forts that were built to guard the city from periodic destruction, especially by the Spanish who objected to the Bahamian wreckers and pirates making off with their goods and treasures, remain. These forts, Montagu to the east, Fincastle above the city, and Charlotte to the west, were built only after the city had been sacked every few years by the Spanish, the French, and even twice by the Americans in some of the first naval activities of the revolutionary war. Oddly, only one of these forts ever fired a shot. Fort Montagu fired four warning shots when the Americans invaded in 1776, but the fort was in such a state of disrepair that two of the shots knocked the cannon off their carriages and the fort fell, as it had several times before, without another sound. The only time that Nassau prepared for an invasion was in 1793 when the forts were readied and the people armed against a French attack that never came.

On July 10, 1973 the stadium and field adjacent to Fort Charlotte was the site where the British flag was lowered for the last time and the flag of the new nation of The Bahamas was raised for the first time. Today the fort has been re-built to its original elegance and grandeur and offers a spectacular view of Nassau Harbour and Independence Field.

The most frequently visited fort is Fort Fincastle which can be seen on the hill above town. Though not large, it is interesting in that it was designed and built in a shape that is reminiscent of a paddle wheel steamer, yet another reminder of the loyalists. Just behind the fort is the water tower. Though not of the loyalist period it does give a fine view of the city below especially in spring and summer when the poinciana, or flame trees, are in bloom and the whole city is ablaze with brilliant red flowers. Just to the east of the water tower is the Queen's Staircase. The 66 steps and the accompanying canyon were cut by slaves in 1793; an amazing feat. The canyon, so narrow that the trees grow over the chasm, is almost completely obscured from above. This makes it cool and shady for the vendors who have souvenir tables for the people who use that route to visit the fort and water tower above.

Banking

Today in Nassau there are no more invasions and there are no more pirates, but the city still depends on

THE STATUE ERECTED TO COMMEMORATE WOODES ROGERS, THE FIRST GOVERNOR.

the sea as much as it ever did. The second largest industry in The Bahamas is overseas banking and investment. The sea, while not absolutely necessary to the venture, divides The Bahamas from the rest of the world giving the investors the freedom to invest in the tax free manner that they desire. Over four hundred major banks and countless investment firms now do business out of The Bahamas. It is in the primary industry, tourism, however, that the sea again takes on a major role. Without the sea there would be sand and sun, but no tourists.

Tourism

Tourism in The Bahamas began with the arrival in 1851 of the first steamship on the New York to Nassau route. The Bahamas as a tourist destination was not popular and the route was abandoned. Tourism started in earnest when the United States imposed prohibition in 1920. Suddenly, The Bahamas became the place for a dry American public to go to for a drink. The town boomed with rum runners, who were using the islands as a base to circumvent the laws, and with rich and thirsty people looking for a drink and a vacation. For a few years tourism flourished and hotels, like the Hotel Colonial, the predecessor to the Sheraton British Colonial Hotel of today, and the Montagu Hotel, which has housed royalty and the famous, were built. Also built was the Bahamian Club which was the first gambling club in Nassau. But, as suddenly as the prosperity had come, it disappeared when, in 1933, prohibition was repealed. The memories of grand days in Nassau survived, however, waiting for a better time.

That day came in the 1960s when the American public started looking for somewhere close, easy to get to, and tropical for their vacations. Almost immediately tourism in The Bahamas boomed again. This boom, bigger now than ever before, is what places Nassau on every map around the globe as one of the world's great vacation destinations. It is Nassau as the international playground that gives the Nassau of today its bright lights and glitter.

Tourists throng the streets of Nassau. Some come into town from the surrounding resorts, but many come off the great, ever-present luxury cruise ships that are docked at Prince George Wharf. Bay Street, the main street near the waterfront, is crowded with people busy seeing the town or shopping in the boutiques that line the street where the highest class, and priced, names like 'Gucci' are right next door to quaint local shops. Also on Bay Street is the Straw Market where handicrafts and souvenirs of every imaginable description are sold. There is no need to walk or drive along the whole of Bay Street as there are colourful horse-drawn carriages.

To the east of town is the small island of Potters Cay. It is there that the fishermen return to sell their catches at the small fish market. Potters Cay is also the home port of the 'mailboat' fleet. These small cargo ships make weekly runs to the Family Islands carrying cargo, passengers and, of course, the mail. For the traveller on a budget, or in search of adventure, the mailboats are an excellent way to get around the islands.

The under-sea life, as always, is one of the major draws for the visitor. The adventurous can contact any one of a dozen dive operations that can be found in Nassau. The area around New Providence Island abounds with exciting and interesting dives. Scuba diving is available on the reefs such as Goulding Cay, at the west end of the island, which once wrecked treasure ships. The myriads of colourful fish are there to watch while you seek your own underwater treasure. Other popular dive opportunities are on the locations of the many films made in The Bahamas. These include the James Bond films *Thunderball*, *Never Say Never*, and *For Your Eyes Only*. There are other locations which have been used in television shows such as *Flipper* and many other movies including *Splash*, *Cocoon*, and *Jaws IV*. Other dives that are available include a blue hole near the east end of the island and wall dives with sea wonders that can hardly be imagined. Further out on the bank and in the Tongue of the Ocean (a deep water canyon which separates New Providence from Andros) are incredible shark dives.

For those who are not quite that adventurous, but who still want to see the treasures of the Bahamian sea, the place to go is Arawak Cay, the man-made cay to the west of town. Scattered throughout the dense shrubbery and flowering gardens are the pools and tanks of Coral World. Coral World is an excellent way to see the marine wonders of the sea without getting wet. Highlights are the reef exhibit, a circular tank that surrounds a room anyone would like to have as their living room, the marine gardens, and the underwater observatory which takes visitors below sea-level for an under-harbour view of the open sea. Coral World is certainly one of the few aquariums in the world to offer such a view. Nearby are Ardastra Gardens where, within a lush tropical park, visitors get as close as they want to the marching flamingos. Iguanas, other reptiles and birds are exhibited in cages.

Surrounding the city of Nassau, the island of New Providence has distinct areas. Eastern Road is an old residential area where the first developers of Nassau, the Bay Street Boys, built large colonial homes that still stand today. In the centre is the over-the-hill district with its small shops and neighbourhood feel. This, the working class district, was the area where many of today's most prominent Bahamians were raised. To the west and south beyond these areas are the wild areas of New Providence island where the coppice scrub, pine barrens, and mangroves beckon to bird watchers and explorers looking for hints of the Lucayans who once lived on the island, or just for a little peace and quiet.

Civilisation is slowly entering these areas. On the far west end of the island is Lyford Cay. Behind the guards and gates is one of the wealthiest and most exclusive residential areas in The Bahamas. Nearby is the more relaxed Love Beach residence and Gambier Village, a small town similar in looks to the Family Island settlements. Around the point is the sumptuous Old Fort Bay where dolphins and manta rays still come into its naturally protected harbour. The Old Fort has stood there since 1723. From the sea it is completely camouflaged by an enormous silk cotton tree a few centuries older than itself.

OVERLOOKING THE CITY OF NASSAU IS GOVERNMENT HOUSE.

This ancient tree and the abandoned building stand firm at the end of New Providence's finest uninhabited beach. Preservation of the Old Fort and its surrounding environment is an essential step in safeguarding one of the few parts of the island's natural heritage which still remain. Further south on the island is Divi, which advertises 'barefoot elegance'. Divi is the only large resort area on the south side of the island and offers scuba diving and golf.

There are two main resort areas in Nassau today. One is west of town in an area called Cable Beach after the first cable radio transmission that was received in the islands. It is now called the 'Bahamian Riviera'. Along the several miles of beach are the Ambassador, Nassau Beach and Royal Bahamian hotels and the ultra-new show case of the Caribbean, the glittering Crystal Palace. The five brightly coloured towers of the Crystal Palace make it the largest hotel/resort complex in the entire Caribbean, and one of the largest in the world. It has 1560 rooms, a 30,000 square foot casino, an 800-seat theatre, a two storey disco, 13 restaurants, and just about every possible variety of sports and recreational opportunity that can be imagined.

When people go on vacation they want to go to paradise, and in Nassau paradise is not only possible, but it is actually there. By crossing the bridge that arches high over Potters Cay the vacationer comes down again in

Paradise Island, the second largest and most glamorous resort area of Nassau.

Paradise Island was called Hog Island until 1961 when it was bought by American millionaire Huntington Hartford and renamed. Over the next few years the island was changed from a quiet offshore cay to one of the world's great tourist destinations. There are five resort hotels on the island offering every luxury to the vacationer. Casinos, stables, pools and a golf course that challenges tour professionals are present on the island. For the quieter moments an eleventh century cloister was transported to the island and rebuilt in the 'Versailles Garden'.

The oldest international airline in the world, 'Chalks' has been landing in Nassau harbour since the First World War. Known today as Paradise Island Airways, visitors winging their way in will be greeted by recently completed new airport facilities. Near to the airport is Hurricane Hole Marina, home to expensive motor yachts. The main draw on the island, as throughout The Bahamas, is the beautiful Cabbage Beach on the north of the island.

BAY STREET, THE HEARTBEAT OF NASSAU.

THE STATUE OF QUEEN VICTORIA AND THE HOUSE OF ASSEMBLY ON RAWSON SQUARE.

A GLASS-BOTTOM BOAT
IN NASSAU HARBOUR.

TRADITIONAL WOODEN SLOOPS
ANCHORED OFF NASSAU. THEIR
ELEGANT LINES ARE STILL A MAJOR
ELEMENT OF THE NASSAU SCENE.

(TOP) MAILBOATS, WHICH CARRY SUPPLIES TO ALL THE MAJOR FAMILY ISLANDS, START FROM POTTERS CAY DOCK IN NASSAU.

(BOTTOM) PRINCE GEORGE WHARF, THE DESTINATION OF HUNDREDS OF CRUISE SHIPS EACH YEAR.

THE STRAW MARKET ON BAY STREET, NASSAU.

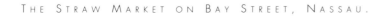

THE PRESTIGIOUS GRAYCLIFF RESTAURANT RETAINS ITS
COLONIAL ELEGANCE.

INSIDE THE BEAUTIFUL
GRAYCLIFF RESTAURANT,
NASSAU.

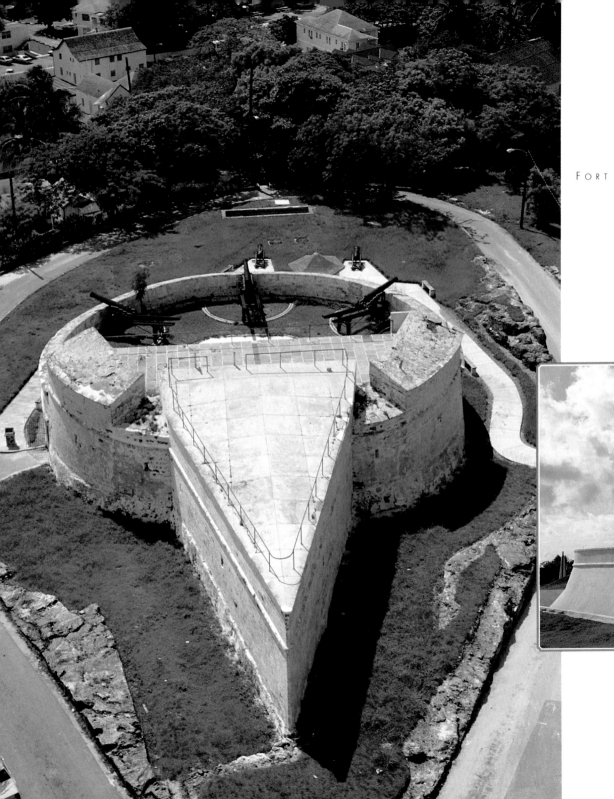

FORT FINCASTLE, NASSAU.

FORT CHARLOTTE, NASSAU.

REFERRED TO AS THE 'WINDOW TO
THE SEA', CORAL WORLD ALLOWS
ONE TO SEE THE UNDERWATER
REALM WITHOUT GETTING WET.

(ABOVE) THE PROTECTED NATURAL HARBOUR
OF OLD FORT BAY, NEW PROVIDENCE.

(RIGHT) LUXURY ON PARADISE ISLAND.

THE WATER TOWER AFFORDS SPECTACULAR VIEWS OF THE PROTECTED CHANNEL BETWEEN NASSAU AND PARADISE ISLAND.

PARADISE ISLAND
AND THE HURRICANE
HOLE MARINA.

GOLFING IN PARADISE.

LOCAL WINDSURFING
CHAMPION, GISELLE
PYFROM.

AN AFTERNOON STROLL
ALONG CABBAGE BEACH
PARADISE ISLAND.

Grand Bahama and Freeport

Sharing the shallow waters of the Little Bahama Bank with the island of Abaco, Grand Bahama boasts the second largest urban centre of The Bahamas at Freeport, which thrives on a continuous flow of tourists. Apart from Freeport and a handful of smaller settlements scattered along the 65-mile coast, Grand Bahama is covered with a vast Caribbean pine forest. A lumbering industry existed here in the 1950s, and at the time employed more people than any other business in The Bahamas.

The Caribbean pine, unlike the introduced Australian casuarina pine, which dominates all The Bahama islands and in many cases has become a menace to the native vegetation, is only found on the islands of Abaco, Andros, New Providence and Grand Bahama.

It was this slender fire-resistant pine that brought hope to this once unknown island, both through foresting and the man who took on the operation. American financier Wallace Groves, who had previously been involved with timbering in the United States, bought the lumber operation at Pine Ridge from the Roberts family in the late 1940s. Groves, who had a reputation for restoring life to dying businesses, proved himself again as he found ways to make the operation profitable. The Pine Ridge project represented the beginning of a concrete development for Grand Bahama. Soon after its inception, Groves started planning his dream – a new city.

Freeport was born from nothing and it was prompted by Grand Bahama's lack of a natural harbour. The island's close proximity to major shipping lanes was an obvious advantage; bearing this in mind, Groves' intention was to create an industrial haven where goods could be imported and sold without any taxes being levied – a free port.

What followed was the most important step for the future of the island. On August 4, 1955, the Hawksbill Creek Agreement was signed between Groves' new company, the Grand Bahama Port Authority, and the Bahamian government. The Bahamas, then under British rule, would hand over Crown land to this private organisation, which agreed in return to take all responsibility for appropriate developments, most significantly the construction of a new harbour.

Although successful in dredging the harbour at the southern mouth of Hawksbill Creek, the Port Authority had trouble attracting potential investors, who shied away from putting their money into an island without any infrastructure. Further amendments were made to the Hawksbill Creek Agreement and shortly afterwards the Port Authority began constructing roads, an airport, a school and a housing project for all the incoming residents. Under Groves' guidance, Freeport began to flourish and within a few years the Port Authority had licensed a number of businesses including hotels and restaurants, a casino, an oil refinery, a cement plant, a chemical factory, farming projects, a milk plant, a bottling company and other smaller operations. Freeport became a city and Wallace Groves' dream came true.

While many of these operations still exist today, it is tourism that reigns in Freeport. The town of Freeport and the suburban neighbourhoods of Lucaya have the appearance of an American metropolis, lacking the typical old charm of other Bahamian locales, yet there are a number of reasons why tourism works here. Miles of white powdery sand beaches, comfortable hotel rooms, two gambling casinos, international restaurants, modern stores, convenient yachting marinas and world class scuba diving make it an ideal spot for the sun-starved vacationer to visit and enjoy.

Established in 1967, the International Bazaar is one of the most popular tourist attractions. A bright red Japanese style Torii gate sits at the entrance of the complex, which consists of stores and restaurants with merchandise and cuisine from around the world. Twenty years later, Port Lucaya began competing with the Bazaar.

Port Lucaya, with a variety of stores and restaurants, overlooks the marina and man-made canals of Lucaya. UNEXCO, thought of as one of the most sophisticated and best equipped diving facilities in the world, is located there.

The first beach-front hotel and casino was built near Port Lucaya. Unlike other soaringly impressive resorts such as the Princess Hotel and Xanadu Beach, the Lucayan Beach Hotel and Casino is a modest three-storey establishment. There are a number of other places to stay in Freeport which may not have the grandeur and luxury of the Lucayan Beach, but which will suit every taste.

In the heart of Lucaya is the famous Garden of The Groves, a landscaped tropical garden with paths winding past lakes, waterfalls and an assortment of native plants and trees. The gardens were created in honour of Mr and Mrs Wallace Groves and overlooking the lush vegetation is a replica of the non-denominational chapels the Groves had built both in Pine Ridge and Little Whale Cay (Berry Islands). A museum depicting Grand Bahamas' history is also set in the gardens.

Adjacent to the gardens is the beautiful 18-hole Shannon Golf and Country Club, one of a handful of golf courses found in Freeport/Lucaya.

While tourism is important in Freeport, its other industries are not far behind. Syntex, a large chemical and pharmaceutical company began operations in 1967 and continues to upgrade and increase the size of its plant. The oil refining and cement companies, which each made their debut in the early days of development, still prosper today. Grand Bahama's exports also include beverages, agricultural and dairy products and the maricultured tilapia fish, all of which leave the island through Freeport's deep water harbour. With a depth of 30 feet at mean low water, the harbour has nine wharfs which load and offload not only merchandise but also the tourists who come on luxurious cruise liners. The private harbour is one of the largest in the world.

The industries of centrally located Freeport/Lucaya only represent a part of Grand Bahama. On either side, the tranquil atmospheres of the settlements are a refreshing contrast.

West End, located on the westerly tip of Grand Bahama, is the oldest and once the largest community of the island and is still nominally the capital of Grand Bahama. The town is laid out in typical island style, with one road inland and the other hugging the shore. The latter, Front Street, has the majority of the stores, restaurants, guest houses and government buildings, while most of the homes are along the inland road. Located on Front Street is the Star Club Restaurant and Bar where the visitor can get a taste of the past and their specialty, the 'sexy conch salad'. Its owner, former senator the Honourable Austin Grant, will relate stories of West End and express his desire to strengthen a town which has experienced a series of booms and busts. Grant's Scottish great-great-grandfather was shipwrecked on a reef and settled here. He explains how his ancestors first survived from cultivating the sisal plant, when land could be purchased at four shillings per acre. Production went up to 1,000 tons a year and ended when a much more lucrative business arose. During the prohibition era West End was known as a bootlegging capital, and large corrugated tin warehouses were built to store the liquor. Grant describes this era, known as the rum-running days: *The Americans came over in their own boats and small planes, picked up their cargo and smuggled it into the U.S.A. They had many a shoot out with the US Coast Guard on the high seas between here and Florida. Many lives were lost and millions of dollars were made. West End was a hard, gay, high-living fun town. Party girls came from Nassau and wherever. Many people made their fortune and went on to further success and many wound up broke. When it was all over the big Bay Street merchants who made their fortunes went back to Nassau and developed a new Bay Street. West End was left in the dumps.*

During the Second World War West End experienced another prosperous period when multimillionaire Alex Wenner-Gren established a canning factory for crawfish and tuna. Overnight this successful industry collapsed when the Swedish entrepreneur fled in his yacht *Southern Cross* after being suspected of collaborating with the Nazis. The old stone canning house still remains next to the Star Club.

This 'boom and bust' history of West End recurred in the late 1940s when Sir Billy Butlin was encouraged by the Bahamian government to build a vacation village here. Shortly after the completion of the project, the British pound devaluated sharply and the Butlin venture went bankrupt. West End became a ghost town again.

The Jack Tar Village, featuring a modern marina, hotel and golf course, has kept a steady flow of business in West End since 1958. But through all its ups and downs, the

West Enders who have maintained the greatest stability are the fishermen.

West End is one of the few places left in The Bahamas where active, old-time bully-net fishermen are to be found. Bully-netting is a traditional method of crawfishing employed by fishermen at the beginning of the industry (1930). Wooden boats are usually manned by two men equipped with a glass-bottom bucket, a tickler and the bully-net. The glass-bottom bucket is used to scan the area and locate the spiny lobsters. Usually, when the crustacean is spotted, only the antennae or feelers are seen protruding from underneath the rock. At this point, one man will grab the tickler, which consists of a curved metal rod attached to one end of a long wooden pole, and prod inside the hole or crevice to push the spiny lobsters out and enable the bully-net to scoop them from the bottom. While one man attempts to capture the crawfish, the other sculls or poles the vessel into position over the coral ledge.

Between West End and the eastern tip of mainland Grand Bahama are several settlements, including Holmes Town, Smith's Point, Deadman's Reef, High Rock, McCleans Town and Eight Mile Rock, the largest settlement outside Freeport. Its proximity to the industrial city has led to its growth, as most of its residents are employed there.

On the other end of the scale, Water Cay, a small settlement separated from the mainland, has dwindled to only a handful of loyal residents. It is situated in the northern backbone of Grand Bahama, an area far away from the commercial centre. It consists primarily of low-lying mangrove islands surrounded by very shallow water.

There are nevertheless people who at weekends commute by boat from Freeport to see their family and savour a few days in this peaceful hideaway.

Sweetings Cay is located in one of the numerous mangrove creeks of eastern Grand Bahama where its residents mostly survive by collecting conch. In the summer, residents of Sweetings Cay and neighbouring McCleans Town join together in a popular conch cracking contest. The objective is to see who can remove the most conchs from their pink shells in a set time. For visitors and locals alike, bonefishing is a popular sport and a fishing lodge has been established on nearby Deep Water Cay.

The creeks surrounding Sweetings and Deep Water Cay are dotted with numerous blue holes. Andros has the most extensive subterranean undersea caves, yet Grand Bahama has its own set of fascinating grottoes.

Both eastern Grand Bahama and an area known as Lucayan National Park have been designated as protected underwater sanctuaries where diving is restricted. The Lucayan Park has the longest underwater systems ever explored, stretching six miles. In one of the two caves of the park, skeletal remains of the Lucayan Indians were found in a sink hole known as the Lucayan Indian Burial Ground.

The impression that some Nassauvians and Family Islanders have is that Grand Bahama is a non-Bahamian island. Even though the tourist centres of Freeport and Lucaya may lack the historic charm of Nassau, the beaches and underwater environments that are open to visitors are superb. Grand Bahamians' way of life is very similar to that in any other Bahamian community.

CRAPS – A POPULAR GAMBLING GAME.

PRINCESS CASINO, ONE OF THE BAHAMAS' FOUR MAJOR GAMBLING ESTABLISHMENTS.

(OPPOSITE) THE ENTRANCE TO THE INTERNATIONAL BAZAAR, FREEPORT.

THE NATIVE CARIBBEAN PINE
IS FOUND IN THE NORTHERN
ISLANDS AND WAS ONCE
LOGGED IN GRAND BAHAMA
AND ABACO.

THE GARDEN OF THE GROVES, DEDICATED TO ITS NAMESAKE AND THE
FOUNDER OF MODERN-DAY FREEPORT, SIR WALLACE GROVES.

THE BEAUTIFUL LUCAYAN BEACH IS A TRUE PARADISE.

THE MARINA AT PORT
LUCAYA, GRAND BAHAMA.

PARASAILING, A
POPULAR THRILL FOR
THE TOURISTS.

AT HIS BAR AND RESTAURANT, 'THE STAR', IS THE HONOURABLE AUSTIN GRANT, A PROMINENT FIGURE IN WEST END, GRAND BAHAMA.

Introduction to the Family Islands

North, south, east and west of the commercial centres of Nassau and Freeport are the 698 remaining islands and cays of the estimated seven hundred that make up The Bahamas. Known for years as the Out Islands, these more peaceful isles have now adopted the appropriate name of the Family Islands and, like each member of a family, each principal island has its own distinct character.

The southernmost island of Inagua, which has an abundance of native plants and animals, has the last remaining Bahamian solar salt industry and the largest breeding colony of West Indian flamingos. In the deep waters between Inagua and Mayaguana is Hogsty Reef, one of only two atoll reef formations in the Atlantic Ocean, where scuba diving is superb.

To the north is the Crooked Island District and the surrounding cays. Three times larger than New Providence with thirty times fewer people, this close-knit group of islands maintains a quiet and simple lifestyle. Fishermen sail to the offshore cays of Samana and Plana to strip cascarilla bark (used in the making of Campari liquor) which is brought back with as much fish, conch and land crabs as can fit in the small boats.

Across the treacherous currents of the Crooked Island Passage lies Long Island, where the wildlife thrives both above and below the waters which fringe this slender stretch of land. Groupers, a favourite eating fish, school in thousands during reproduction, and sharks are fed by hand by local experts. Long Islanders are ethnically the most mixed of Bahamians. They depend heavily on fishing and farming but have found time to build some of the fastest regatta boats in The Bahamas.

East of Long Island is the trio of Conception Island, Rum Cay and San Salvador, all separated by deep water passages. The latter has received worldwide attention as the official first landfall of Christopher Columbus in 1492. Archaeological finds in San Salvador and in the caves of Rum Cay are testimony to habitation by Lucayan Indians whom Columbus may have encountered, but unfortunately no concrete evidence exists that proves Columbus actually landed in San Salvador or anywhere else proposed as 'Columbus' first discovery island'.

One contender for the landfall title is nearby Cat Island. While it has not received much recognition as the discovery island, Cat Island, with its rolling hills and miles of untrodden beaches, boasts one of the most attractive landscapes of The Bahamas. Furthermore its people have kept the old traditional 'rake 'n' scrape' music, story telling, farming methods and bush medicine alive.

In this central part of The Bahamas are The Exumas

which consist of two larger islands, Great and Little Exuma, with a chain of nearly two hundred cays, considered by many as the best cruising ground of The Bahamas. Boats from many parts of the world come here for the variety of anchorages, a protected land and sea park, sailboat regattas and wild iguanas.

Iguanas, which are dragon-like reptiles, are also found in other Bahamian islands such as Andros, which is separated from the shallow waters of Exuma by an unusual deep water canyon called the Tongue of the Ocean. Unlike its gregarious neighbour, the Androsian species of iguana is extremely shy and said to measure up to six feet. One that big has never been documented and remains another island myth like the chickarnies, red-eyed animals which supposedly hang from pine trees. Mysterious yet true are the famous blue holes of Andros. These subterranean caves and passages are the most extensive in the world and have recently revealed species thought extinct as well as bones of the earliest native West Indians.

The Family Islands may appear to be a world apart for the casual visitor, yet there are, on every principal island, comfortable places of accommodation and locals who are ready to show a stranger around. With the Exumas, it is the northern islands of Eleuthera, Abaco and Bimini which have the most tourism.

Bimini's close proximity to the United States has, since the days of liquor prohibition, brought visitors to this small island. Today's vacationers, for the most part, come in on large sport-fishing boats to meet the challenge of marlin, tuna and other game fish found in the Gulf Stream. A hundred miles across the Great Bahama Bank from Bimini are the Berry Islands, another very popular fishing ground which, like Bimini, sit on the edge of very deep water and provide excellent scuba diving.

Probably the fastest growing populations in the Family Islands are found in Abaco and Eleuthera; this is undoubtedly linked to tourism. From golfing to shark fishing, these larger islands offer just about everything a visitor wants from a tropical holiday. Tourism, however, is not the only industry practised by Abaconians and Eleutherans; there is also a great reliance on fishing and, to a smaller extent, farming. Communities such as Grand Cays in Abaco and Spanish Wells in Eleuthera have a very successful fishing industry and although they cater well to tourists, they do not rely on them.

A brief introduction to the different groups of islands will only give a hint of the diversity that exists in the Family Islands of The Bahamas. To outsiders and many Bahamians these islands are unknown, but those who have discovered them are left with lasting images of their natural beauty.

THE WELL PROTECTED HARBOUR OF HOPE TOWN, ABACO.

Eleuthera

'Eleuthera' means freedom in Greek, and the first post-Columbus settlers, the small group of Eleutheran Adventurers, an independent company, came to the island in 1648 to find religious freedom above all. Their arrival from Bermuda proved to be disastrous as Captain Sayle and his crew crashed on the Devil's Backbone, located on the northern side of the island. The group of settlers had to adapt to the impoverished soil and hard living conditions. Many died and some went back to their former homes.

Some of today's Eleutherans, primarily from Spanish Wells, Current and Harbour Island, are direct decendants of those first hardy adventurers who learned to farm the land and harvest the sea. Other settlements on the mainland also carry families from the stock of early settlers; overall, however, they were populated in the later years by plantation owners and their slaves, who were better at utilising the land for large and small scale farming operations. Eleuthera has therefore always been one of the most prosperous of the Family Islands both for farming and fishing.

There are many interesting and unique geographic and environmental features throughout the 200-square-mile island. From the north and the fast-moving Current Cut and the treacherous reef of the Devil's Backbone, to the south and the geological phenomena of the 'Glass Window', the deep caves at Hatchet Bay, the inland waterhole in Rock Sound and the isolated cays with their natural richness, there is much to marvel at.

The 106-mile-long island, with its breathtaking shoreline and adjoining cays is only a twenty-minute plane ride or an adventurous half-day cruise on the mailboat away from Nassau.

In North Eleuthera, most of the men work as fishermen out of Current or Spanish Wells and are gone for two to five weeks at a time harvesting conch and crawfish. Current is about half a mile long and is over two hundred years old. Much of the architecture is reminiscent of old New England towns, with small wooden clapboard houses. Some of the early Current settlers had sailed from Scotland roughly 150 years ago to go to America but had, like the first Eleutheran Adventurers, been shipwrecked on the Devil's Backbone reef in North Eleuthera. Both Current and Spanish Wells are thus predominantly white from Loyalist descent.

Spanish Wells with its well-kept houses is very clean, friendly and organised. Spanish Wells is considered by many to be the major centre for crawfishing in The Bahamas. In Spanish Wells fishermen leave on large boats, equipped with smaller fifteen-foot dinghies with outboard engines. The fast, sturdy fibreglass boats move a crew of two or three people in and around the shoals and reef systems. A diver will stay in one area as long as he continues to find crawfish. Sometimes, a diver will work for a couple of hours around a fruitful ledge, stacking crawfish after crawfish on the spare rods. The speed and accuracy involved in gathering the spiny creatures is astounding. The diver wastes no time, for the lobsters are quick to retreat far back in the holes. Surfacing when all the spears are loaded and heavy with shell fish, a diver will stack as many as forty spiny animals on one rod. At the end of a day's work, the fisherman 'wrings' the crawfish, separating the heads from the tails. Most carapaces are thrown into the sea as it is not economically feasible to

process the heads. The highly valued tails are stored in freezers on board, some of which have a capacity of up to 30,000 pounds.

The reef system surrounding North Eleuthera is a haven for beginning and advanced scuba diving. At the famous Current Cut, during periods of peak ebb and flowing tides, the current moves forcefully through the passage at five or six knots. The cut is one of the most popular dive sites in North Eleuthera. Depending upon the tidal movement, divers will enter on one side of the channel and drift dive through the cut as many as four times before exhausting their air supply.

Unlike many other Family Island communities, Harbour Island has a developed tourist industry and many visitors consider it to be one of the most beautiful islands in The Bahamas. Dunmore Town, the island's main settlement, was, until quite recently, The Bahamas' second city after Nassau. From the eighteenth century until the Second World War, it was a ship-building centre; the largest ship ever constructed in The Bahamas, the four-masted *Marie J Thompson*, was built there in 1922. When looking around at the large and small wooden buildings, the old-style houses, the colonial homes, the blossoming gardens, the spectacular pink sand beach, the family establishments, the shops, restaurants and nightclubs, and, of course, the hotels, it is easy to understand why Harbour Island has

THE BRIDGE LINKING CUPID'S CAY WITH GOVERNOR'S HARBOUR.

received so much exposure in magazines and books. A water taxi runs from Harbour Island to the mainland of Eleuthera.

The first communities towards the south are Upper and Lower Bogue. The total population is about 800, but Upper Bogue is the smallest. The Bogue used to be known as the Bog, due to its wet, spongy ground. The low, swampy marshes filled with fish during the hurricane 'Betsy', when the sea flooded the land. This is why an assortment of ocean fish like groupers, snappers and barracudas can still be found in the inland ponds.

East of The Bogues is the Glass Window. This wind- and wave-sculptured formation occurs at Eleuthera's thinnest point, where only a few yards separate the Bahamian bank from the Atlantic Ocean. The Window itself is a natural bridge that opens on both the eastern and western shores of the island. From the bridge on top of the Glass Window, the view is breathtaking. Bluffs overlooking the ocean are 75 to 100 feet above sea-level. Looking to the west, or the Caribbean side, the colour is a light pastel blue and the white sand-covered banks stretch for miles offshore. Looking east, to the Atlantic side, the ocean is a deep blue with frothy white caps.

North Eleuthera is also known for its pineapple industry, where harvests are gathered during both the summer and winter. It is said that the summer crop is sweeter than the winter one because less fertilizer is needed. Gregory Town, the pineapple capital of Eleuthera, is a very picturesque village with a large church at the entrance and houses of different shapes and colours scattered all over the hillside. Before Hawaii took over, The Bahamas had the largest pineapple industry in the world and supplied North America and Europe with fruit. There was a very lucrative canning factory in Gregory

FISHING FOR SHARKS FROM THE CLIFFS IS A POPULAR SPORT IN ELEUTHERA.

Town, but it is no longer of use as the delicious Bahamian pineapples now are grown for local consumption.

Surfer's Beach attracts the special interest visitor to Eleuthera. Near to Gregory Town, along a bushy and bumpy path off the main road, on the Atlantic side, are some of the best waves in The Bahamas.

There are several interesting caves on Eleuthera, especially one close to Hatchet Bay. Along a dusty, red two-track road through tall savannah grass, is the small entrance for the cave. Steps and wooden ladders were placed by bat guano or droppings harvesters who made forays deep into the cavern to accumulate and harvest the guano for use as fertilizer. Bat guano has a very high concentration of nitrogen and is used in garden plots. Aside from the graffiti on the walls, the cave has some spectacular stalagmites and stalactites in all sizes and shapes. Colonies of bats hang from the ceiling and, roughly 2000 feet into the cave, there is water in small

THE WIND- AND WAVE-SCULPTURED FORMATION KNOWN AS THE GLASS WINDOW, ELEUTHERA.

pools. This water is fresh and comes from subterranean pockets of trapped rain water which leak down through the porous limestone.

Between Hatchet Bay and Governor's Harbour Airport is the old settlement of James Cistern. James Cistern was named after the late Governor, Sir James, who served his term at Governor's Harbour. In search of water supplies, Sir James discovered a natural water hole while out riding his horse. The hole was perfectly situated to allow easy transport of water to Governor's Harbour. Soon a cistern was built and the community started to grow around it. Hidden behind the houses are clay 'Dutch' ovens and the smell of burning wood and baking bread wafts throughout the settlement regularly.

Like many other settlements in the Family Islands, Governor's Harbour was at one time a very prosperous trading town. In the 1800s vegetables and fruits were exchanged with United States' companies for construction supplies, tools, clothing and household items. Today, Governor's Harbour is by no means inactive, but is no longer a centre of trade. Governor's Harbour is located right in the middle of Eleuthera. The main road runs all along the hook shaped harbour, while some of the crossroads run up the hill. The international airport for the area is about fifteen minutes away. At the principal intersection of the town is a traffic light, the only one in Eleuthera.

Along Queen's Highway, which is the principal road from the north to the south of the island, are several settlements such as Palmetto Point, Savannah Sound and Tarpum Bay. They are all worth a visit. The largest town on Eleuthera is Rock Sound. At the entrance there is the only modern shopping centre on Eleuthera. A public library, a clinic, government offices and a waterhole, where locals and visitors come to swim, can be found there.

Eleuthera is also famous for its resorts. Windermere Island is connected to the mainland by bridge, and is a favourite vacation spot for the British royal family. The Club has a gorgeous view of the Atlantic and many exclusive properties. The Cotton Bay Beach and Golf Club is the most complete luxury resort on southern Eleuthera, with a Robert Trent Jones 18-hole golf course that stretches around the beach, ponds and tropical vegetation.

The southernmost portion of Eleuthera looks like the tail of a whale. At one tip, Powell Point opens the coastline to the sound, and on the other end of the tail is the southern tip. It is a spectacular spot with a large pink sand beach surrounded by tall cliffs and rock formations. There is also a small lighthouse perched on the highest part of the cliff. Between the two points are a series of small communities: Deep Creek, Delancey Town, Waterford, Wemyss Bight, Millars, Bannerman Town and Green Castle. From the tall cliffs at the southern point of Eleuthera it is possible to see, twelve miles to the east, the uninhabited island of Little San Salvador.

Abaco and its Cays

Abaco is the second largest Bahamian island. On its windward side, a continuous chain of cays extends as far north as the Matanilla reef which marks the top of the Little Bahama Bank. The mainland begins in the south at Hole In The Wall and ends at Crown Haven on Little Abaco. The land mass between the two points is at its widest ten miles, with sections of land thinning to a stone's throw from either side. At one time, Abaco was probably broken into smaller islands which, over time with the help of mangroves and the build-up of limestone, have joined into one Abaco island.

Shaped like a long, bent arm, the area around the 'elbow' is known as the Hub of Abaco and comprises Marsh Harbour, Hope Town and Man-O-War Cay. The principal town of Marsh Harbour is the largest town in Abaco and the third largest town in the Family Islands. The facilities here are exceptionally modern and the department stores, boutiques and restaurants seem almost out of place in such tranquil islands. With so much development, Marsh Harbour attracts 'commuters' from all over the neighbouring cays.

The two other communities forming the Hub Of Abaco are Man-O-War Cay and Hope Town on Elbow Cay, each located on separate islands opposite busy Marsh Harbour. In the 'Hub', where a small boat acts like a car,

locally built work boats ply back and forth between the communities all day long.

Hope Town, famous for its candy-striped lighthouse, its historical museum and relaxed atmosphere, attracts many visitors. Most of the original settlers came from the Carolinas in the late 1700s to show their continued loyalty to the British Crown. They hoped to reproduce their southern plantations but discovered that harvesting fish from the sea was more profitable. Their descendants have prospered most recently through tourism, developing comfortable hotels, numerous rental cottages, bars and restaurants. With its extremely sheltered harbour, Hope Town has for many years been a popular stop over for yachtsmen. The cruising boat regatta, 'Regatta Time in Abaco', is in early July and starts here; it comprises a series of short races taking the boats on a competitive island hop of the Abacos. Dominating the scene is the old lighthouse, the building of which was opposed by residents in the late 1800s. Hope Town was a centre for wrecking at that time, and any aid to marine safety was certainly unwelcome.

Man-O-War Cay is just north of Hope Town; it is striking in its extreme tidiness, making Hope Town seem like something of an unruly cousin. The island feels like a freshly painted boat, a spin off from the dominant occupation. Man-O-War is famed for its high quality wooden and, more recently, fibreglass boats. The skilled craftsmen have attracted customers from the United States to have their boats refitted here.

South of the Hub is the main land mass of Abaco. Here are the forests of slender pines which used to form the basis of Abaconian income. At the turn of the century, lumber yards, roads and settlements for construction workers were developed by American investors. The industry moved to Grand Bahama in the 1950s, the villagers reverting to the traditional occupations of fishing and farming. The now peaceful pine forests, crisscrossed with disused lumber tracks, are home to the Bahama parrot. Frightened by the lumber industry and attacked by wild dogs and cats, the parrot population was in jeopardy.

TREASURE CAY ABACO.

Protection measures, including large fines, have helped save the birds, which are particularly vulnerable since they nest in holes in the limestone, right at ground level.

On the southernmost point of the Little Bahama Bank and of Abaco is the Hole In The Wall lighthouse. From the top of the ninety-three-foot tower there is a splendid view of the large ocean vessels crossing the Northeast Providence channel. Apart from the lighthouse there is the 'hole in the wall' itself – a large natural perforation at the end of a huge rock platform. On the south-western tip, Sandy Point is a remote community and Crossing Rocks to the north-east shares its traditional style and way of life. For remoteness however, Moore's Island, nestling in the edge of the Bight of Abaco, is unmatched. A hardy black community, the island is remarkable for the women who play a major role in the subsistence level of fishing and farming.

Back on the eastern edge of Abaco, the all-white community of Cherokee Sound, once a thriving boat-building centre, now bases its economy on construction work and other skilled labour in nearby Marsh Harbour. Sharing the same small peninsula is Little Harbour, an artist's sanctuary. The studio of sculptor Ran Johnston is fascinating. Many of his bronze works stand in important town squares of The Bahamas.

North of the Hub, the communities are far more influenced by tourism than in the south. Great Guana Cay, once called Foot Cay due to its shape, is the largest of the Abaco Cays and has the most gorgeous beaches. Sea turtles come every spring to lay their eggs in the soft sand. At the Guana Beach Resort, T-shirts state 'It's better in The Bahamas but Gooder in Guana'.

The Albert Lowe Museum in New Plymouth, the only settlement on Green Turtle Cay, exhibits a collection of

A NATURAL SAND HIGHWAY, EXPOSING ITS SPARKLING SURFACE, CAN CHANGE SHAPE AND FORM
WITH EACH FLOWING TIDE (GREEN TURTLE CAY, ABACO).

paintings, sculptures and wooden ship models that describe the history of Abaco. Famous painter Alton Lowe and sculptor James Mastin both have a remarkable assemblage of their work in the museum. A variety of little bars in New Plymouth attracts many local Abaconians from the other cays. The nearby peninsula on Abaco has also been tastefully developed; the entire bay at Treasure Cay is beautiful and the facilities for yachtsmen are particularly good. It is believed that the first Loyalist settlement of Abaco, called Carlton, was established here in 1783, at the western point of the bay. It was unknown until 1979, when archaeologists unearthed artefacts.

Further up the island and its string of cays, the tourist activity dies out. The land narrows to a thin strip, tipped by Little Abaco with its many small communities; Cooper's Town, Cedar Harbour, Wood Cay, Mount Hope, Fox Town, and Crown Haven. The towns are seldom marked on the maps but their people best represent the traditional black Abaconian lifestyle. The concept of generation property still exists here, and consequently the land has remained in the care of the few families that carry on the traditions of their fathers. Their wooden boats can be seen sculling inside the shallow Bight of Abaco. Cisterns for rain collection and wells supply water to the homes, and some families have their own generators.

Away from the mainland into the long chain of cays to the north-west, people and settlements become fewer and further between. The residents of Stranger's Cay and Carter Cay collectively total not more than twenty individuals. These people are all fishermen. Outside the crawfish season they will gather conch and catch scalefish.

Further away from civilisation, a string of uninhabited cays lead to Walker's and Grand Cays, the northernmost settlements. Typically, man has made his mark at the furthest point of the chain, the most northerly point in the whole of The Bahamas. Walker's is an exclusive resort and marina for sport-fishermen who ply the rich waters for billfish, wahoo, dorado and other game. At the western end of the 100-acre island is a unique aquaculture farm, one of the few mass breeding farms for tropical fish in the world.

Six miles south-east, Grand Cay is as traditional as Walker's is sophisticated. The inhabitants are hardworking fishermen, who hold an annual conch cracking contest in July. In these parts of the Abacos and further out on the Little Bahama Bank, dolphins have become extremely friendly with boaters. Large groups of spotted dolphins swim with divers for hours. These sociable mammals are a symbol of the grace and beauty of their environment.

THE FAMOUS CANDY-STRIPED LIGHTHOUSE AT HOPE TOWN, ABACO.

Bimini

On the edge of the Gulf Stream, only fifty miles from Miami, is Bimini, the big-game fishing capital of the world. Currents in the Gulf Stream bring up rich plankton from deep waters, which in turn attract a multitude of fish, including blue marlin, tuna and wahoo. Many world record fish have been caught close to Bimini. In the mid-1930s, Ernest Hemingway lived in Bimini, encouraging the sport which has made the island so famous.

Bimini is actually not just one island, but a gentle curve of islands, cays and rocks which run from north to south along the 'drop off', where depths plummet from a few to thousands of feet. The main island, North Bimini, is a long thin strip of land only seven miles long and seven hundred yards wide at its widest point. This is where the majority of Biminites live, where the fishermen come to harbour and an increasing number of tourists stay to relax. South Bimini, once the farming centre of the chain, is home to the main airport and a handful of properties. To the east is an unspoilt system of mangroves and sandy shores, the nursery for an abundance of marine life and a favourite bonefishing ground. To the south lie a series of smaller outcrops known for good fishing and scuba diving, and at the end of the curve an exclusive haven of millionaire homes and gardens nestles

amongst the elegant palms of Cat Cay.

Bimini's close proximity to mainland America has been a major determiner of the islanders' fortune and fate through the centuries. The first European visitor to the Bimini islands was Ponce de Léon, who set out to establish a colony in the name of King Ferdinand of Spain in 1513. After a search for the 'Fountain of Youth', reputedly located on South Bimini, Ponce de Léon made for the Florida coast, hoping to settle the area. By the mid-1800s, a few families of West African ancestry had made their way to the shores of Bimini. Newly freed from servitude, these families scraped a living from the land and sea. South Bimini was used as farmland, while North Bimini, with its clear view of the shipping lanes, was better suited for habitation, as the new settlers were ever hopeful of locating wrecked cargo ships along the treacherous reefs. In fact, the strong Gulf currents and occasional storms brought so many ships to the nearby reefs that prospective wreckers from Grand Bahama migrated there.

Over the years, Biminites have involved themselves in sponging, shell collection, conching and fishing as well as other 'innocent' land based endeavours such as the growing of sisal for rope. However, their returns from such traditional labours were miniscule compared to the profits from more shady pursuits. During the American

Civil War, Biminites worked as blockade runners to bring supplies to the South, and in the 1920s, prohibition turned Bimini into the headquarters for rum runners. The short run to Florida was a natural attraction as fast sailing boats laden with barrels of illicit alcohol set out from Bimini to rendezvous with fast motor boats which dodged Customs vessels to supply thirsty Florida and beyond. As well as taking liquor to the States, Biminites attracted Americans to the island. To cater for the sudden boom in visitors, the Bimini Bay Rod and Gun Club was built; a huge 165-room hotel featuring a casino and ballroom. Another major attraction of Bimini during this era was the 2,700 ton concrete ship, *Sapona*, which acted as a floating private club and bootleg liquor cache. Unfortunately, the

THE CRYSTAL CLEAR WATERS OF BIMINI REVEAL HOW THE DEPTH CHANGES.

THE CHALKS AIRLINE REMAINS THE LONGEST RUNNING INTERNATIONAL AIR SERVICE IN THE
WORLD, AND LINKS BIMINI, NASSAU AND MIAMI.

Rod and Gun Club was devastated by the hurricane of 1926 and the *Sapona* was blown aground by another storm in 1929. Sadly for Biminites, who had become reliant on the boot-legging trade, their livelihood disappeared with the repeal of the Prohibition Act in 1933.

One bonus from the sudden prohibition-related investment interest in Bimini was the establishment of the seaplane service. 'Pappy' Chalk set up a Miami-Bimini flight in 1919, landing right in the calm harbour of North Bimini Bay. Now the longest running international airline in the world, Chalks still connects North Bimini with Florida and Nassau. The daily arrival of Chalks is a great occasion as the plane splashes down and majestically rolls right up on to land, across the main road and to a stop in Alice Town.

In the 1970s, Bimini gained a reputation for drug smuggling. With its past history and ideal location, this perhaps was a natural progression. Present-day Bimini has been cleaned up by the joint efforts of the Bahamian and American authorities, and with a healthy tourist and sport-fishing industry, Bimini seems to be in a state of happy stability. The ups and down of the past have made Biminites particularly adaptable and this may be one reason that they cater so well to present-day tourist needs.

All the main amenities of Bimini lie along a short stretch of road between Chalks and the all-age school in Alice Town. Small bars, restaurants and shops trail along the dusty highway, right next to beautiful Bimini Bay, with its shallow conch beds and view of East Bimini's dense mangroves where the unusual sulphurous springs have become a popular healing source. The bayside has several docking facilities, usually lined with an impressive array of visiting luxury fishing boats and yachts. Not so luxurious but highly reliable is the 100-foot *Bimini Mack*, the mailboat which carries anything from cars to ice-cream from Nassau and Miami. The western shore provides a different picture; a seemingly endless white sand beach is all that lies between the thin ridge of land and the deep blue Gulf Stream.

Ossie Brown's Compleat Angler Hotel, one of the first fishing clubs in The Bahamas when it was built in the early 1930s, is an inevitable stop while in North Bimini. Inside, along the varnished wooden walls, are countless pictures depicting the past fifty or so years of Bimini's enduring character. Glorious black and white prints of huge tuna and marlin dragged from the Gulf Stream, accompanied by many of Hemingway's timeless passages, transport visitors back to the romance and excitement of those early fishing championships. North of Alice Town and its commercial centre, the road meanders into Bayley Town, the residential area where most Biminites live. Beyond this are a few tranquil retreats. The late congressman Adam Clayton Powell had a second home here, as did former inventor and avid fisherman George Albert Lyon. Perched on top of the rocks of Paradise Point, Lyon built a dream house with superb views. The point looks out over clear waters beneath which lie unusual 'roads' of symmetrical rocks.

Called 'Bimini Wall', 'Bimini Roads', 'The Sunken City', or just 'Atlantis', the site itself was first discovered in 1968 by explorer Dr J. Manson Valentine, and first scientifically surveyed beginning in 1969 by Dimitri Rebikoff. After years of photographic mapping and boring operations it has been proposed by Valentine, Rebikoff and some geologists that the 'sunken walls, piers or buildings' are the work of man. Carbon dating suggests a date of submergence about 11,000 years ago. The presence of these enormous blocks and the unusual healing waters found on East and South Bimini have led to much speculation. Was Bimini the site of the ancient city of Atlantis? Were Ponce de Léon's beliefs in the Fountain of Youth not as far fetched as many think? The questions are still there and so is Bimini with its rough diamond character and unique charms.

The Berry Islands

The thirty small islands that make up the Berrys lie only 35 miles from New Providence and are at a comfortable distance for Bahamians to use as a weekend fishing ground. The Great Bahama Bank, on which this delicate curve of islands sits, is plentifully stocked with good eating fish. Local favourites are grouper, snapper, hogfish and triggerfish, to name but a few. Sport-fishermen, motivated by the chase more than hunger, also come from Florida for marlin, bluefin tuna and other spirited breeds. Many of them stay overnight at the semi-private Chub Cay Club on the southernmost island.

Only five hundred people live in the Berrys, most of them based on Great Harbour Cay. Originally settled by ex-slaves in the mid 1800s, it now caters to passing yachtsmen with a fuel station, stores and a clinic. Between Great Stirrup Cay in the north and Chub Cay in the south are several island homes which, for the owners, are the resolution of some life-long yearning. Interestingly, Wallace Groves, the pioneer of Freeport's development, had his private island paradise here on Little Whale Cay. The beautifully kept hideaways, with their own docks, pools, tennis courts, and, in some cases runways, are neighbours to the pelicans, noddies and terns which nest on the untamed cays that preserve the windswept charm of this idyllic cluster of islets.

HOOKING A DOLPHIN FISH, ONE OF THE SPIRITED GAMEFISH FOUND IN THE DEEP WATERS OFF THE BERRY ISLANDS

MAN AGAINST FISH – MARLIN FISHING OFF BIMINI

Sand banks in the Berry Islands.

The Exumas

The Exuma Cays and Great and Little Exuma make up a chain of over two hundred fascinating islands, where the sunlit ocean graduates from soft mint greens to the shimmering blues of turquoise and teal. The northern Exumas are probably one of the finest showcases of natural marine beauty in the world.

The Exumas begin actually at Sail Rocks, about 35 miles south-east of Nassau. The trip from the capital is a colourful one, as the shallow sands are peppered with coral heads across the aptly named Yellow Banks. The first landfall is Allan's Cay, where the residents are two feet long and crawling on the beach. The rock iguana, or Bahamian dragon, is the local host for boat-people entering the Exuma chain at Allan's Cay. Appearing to be shipwrecked survivors from prehistoric times, the iguanas are far from shy; they stroll forcefully down to the water line as inquisitive boaters approach, ready for any scraps that might be thrown their way.

At the heart of the chain is the Exuma Cays Land and Sea Park, a 176-square-mile protected sanctuary. The park begins at Wax Cay Cut and extends 22 miles south-east to Conch Cut. The rules are 'you can see but don't take'. This prudent measure will ensure the continued abundance of marine life throughout the islands, since heavy overfishing was beginning to threaten populations.

To the north of the park, Highbourne Cay is the main inhabited island, its tall mast being a guide to shipping from Nassau. Boaters can fuel up and buy food here. Nearby, Norman's Cay has a scattering of now derelict luxury homes along its shores. The former headquarters of a drug baron, Norman's has now been left to the birds and occasional barefoot sailors.

Just south of the park is Staniel Cay, a thriving community with much to commend it. At certain times of the year this quiet and charming island becomes a hub of activity. The annual Bonefishing Festival in the summer and the New Year's Day Cruising Regatta are two of those times. Generally, visitors come by boat since the island caters to cruisers with good dock facilities, but there is also a 3000-foot airport and charter service. On the southern part of the island are several beautiful homes, mostly built by Americans. Diving is very good around Staniel Cay: just a minute away from the Yacht Club is the famous Thunderball Grotto. This cave has been featured in two James Bond movies and other Hollywood motion films. Light filters through natural holes in the limestone dome, sending shafts of light to the bottom of the clear water to illuminate the many fish below.

Just south of Staniel is Black Point, the largest and perhaps most traditional community in the Exuma chain.

Outwardly this settlement has remained unaffected by tourism and its inhabitants are reliant on fishing, small-scale farming and straw work for the Nassau market. The palmetto palms are grown on the island, dried and stripped into uniform lengths to be deftly woven into long ribbons which in turn can be sewn into hats, mats and baskets.

Beyond is an equally fascinating but smaller community: the narrow entrance of Farmers Cay opens into a cove where the dock is situated. The little village of small wooden houses sits on the side of a hill where tranquillity reigns. No wonder Captain Henry Moxey, one of the finest boat pilots in The Bahamas, decided to retire here. The community consists of elderly and very young people, but the population of less than a hundred rises with the return of the young folk during vacations. Straw working and fishing are the dominant occupations, but pleasure boaters often use the safe harbour and bring in welcome trade. The Farmers Cay First Friday in February Festival, or 5Fs, is an event which has become quite popular with yachtsmen. The 5Fs weekend has races, games, raffles, food, dancing and the only official hermit crab race in The Bahamas.

Dotted along the largely uninhabited central cays of the Exumas are the ruins of past plantations, cattle farms and private homes.

The last cay of the Exuma Cays is Lee Stocking Island where the Caribbean Marine Research Centre is breeding tilapia. Marine biologists are developing ways to raise this prolific freshwater fish in salt water. The purpose of the study is to stock certain areas in the Caribbean, especially some of the depleted fishing grounds off Haiti. The northern part of Great Exuma is being tested as a potential area for release of the fish.

Rolleville in Great Exuma is probably the most populated settlement of the Exumas. There are many rolling hills, and homes of all styles have been built. Joe A. Romer is known as the Medicine Man for the area. He usually comes to most festivities with his special herbs. The plants he uses include five finger, boar bush, love vine, stiff cock, strong back, madeira bark, and lignum vitae. Many of the locals still rely to some extent on traditional bush medicine with local plants being used to cure a broad range of ailments from impotency to asthma.

In the northern part of Great Exuma most of the people are involved in farming and fishing; there are many farming communities such as Moss Town, Steventon and Mount Thompson along the road to Georgetown. Mount Thompson is the farming centre of Exuma. Onions have been an important vegetable for Exuma for a long time and even appear on the Exuma crest. At the beginning of the century, the Commissioner's Report stated that '...for the year 1908, 2000 pounds of onions were grown, equal to 14 barrels. Of that number, 11 barrels were exported and sold for 6 pounds and 10 pence.'

Although farming is still a key industry, tourism is being developed, fortunately at a slow and unobtrusive level. The eastern side of Great Exuma has many beautiful homes along its shore and a new airport brings visitors to George Town with its variety of accommodation.

Elizabeth Harbour, George Town, is probably the largest bay and natural protected area in the entire southern Bahamas. To the east it is protected by the long narrow ridge of Stocking Island, a natural barrier from the ocean with its distinctive cliffs and tower. The harbour is the venue for the biggest and most exciting traditional boat regatta of The Bahamas. The Family Island Regatta is held at the end of April each year. With standing starts

THE EXUMA CAYS LAND AND SEA PARK, A NATURE RESERVE WHERE ALL LIVING THINGS ARE
PROTECTED AND WHERE CRUISING VESSELS WILL FIND A SAFE ANCHORAGE.

and furious competition the wooden sloops are a majestic sight, their gleaming white sails set against the bluest of waters.

George Town can be seen from the sea at quite a distance, primarily because of the pink buildings, of which the Government Administration Building is the largest. It was modelled on Government House in Nassau, and also serves as the post office. In the centre of town is a gigantic tree, where locals shelter from the sun or sell straw work. George Town is a growing community with development plans and forward looking inhabitants. That is not to say there is any lack of charm; the people are friendly and it is easy to engage in conversation or even in a game of basketball.

Just about six miles from George Town, on a hill overlooking the channel between Great and Little Exuma, is Rolletown. The name Rolle has continued through descendants of the slaves owned by early settlers. The otherwise anonymous slaves were given the family name of their 'owner' when purchased.

The Ferry is the first settlement on the north-west tip of Little Exuma, its name coming from the times when there was no bridge connecting Great and Little Exuma. The oldest building in town is as much a museum as a home. Its owners are George and Gloria Patience. She is also known as the 'Shark Lady,' and has hauled in over 1000 sharks, including an 18-foot tiger shark in her 13-foot Boston whaler. She sells the teeth from the sharks she catches and is also an artist, archaeologist and sailor. She has skippered boats in the Family Island Regatta and is famed for her topless, all-female crew.

On the Atlantic side is the small settlement of Forbes Hill, named after early settlers, where most of the community is involved in farming. On a hill nearby is The Fort, the ruins of a fortress which has been apparently in existence since 1892 and was used during the time of British rule. There is a beautiful view for miles and a beach below named 'Fort Bay'. Local legend has it that on moonlight nights a mermaid sits on the shores, combing her hair.

The last community of the Exumas is Williams Town, a clean little town with many old buildings bordered by an abandoned salt lake. At one time the salt industry and the cotton fields employed eight hundred people in the settlement. It is now home to less than a hundred people. The old stone beacon on the cliff once guided ships which picked up salt for export to Nova Scotia and North America.

Ragged Island Chain

Despite their relative closeness to the Exumas, the thin wisp of islands known as Jumentos Cays and Ragged Island Chain are rarely visited by outsiders and unknown to all but a handful of Bahamians. The croissant shaped chain stretches for over 110 miles, tipped at the southern end by Duncan Town, Ragged Island. There are no hotels, but every opportunity to stay with the inhabitants who are always ready to take care of the very few travellers who visit their 'paradise'.

On some of the cays like Racoon Cay, Hog Cay and Double-Breasted Cay, it is possible to spot goats and the ruins of stone pens where they were once contained. Today the goats are wild and are occasionally hunted by the locals. Ragged Islanders are excellent marksmen and will shoot pigeons from their boats.

Duncan Town, the one and only settlement of the entire chain, is situated inside a natural bay of shallow

Elizabeth Harbour and the
popular yachting haven of
George Town, Exuma.

Salt pans at
Ragged Island.

water. Named after Duncan Taylor, who established a salt industry there, most of the inhabitants are the direct descendants of the very first settlers and bear their family names – Maycock, Wallace, Wilson, Munroe, Curling, and Lockhart.

A paradise of reefs and beaches rarely seen and nothing but the sound of the wind, the waves and the wings of birds, Duncan Town and the Ragged Island Chain are remote and beautiful.

WOVEN FROM THE DRIED LEAVES OF LOCAL PALMETTO PALMS, STRAW WORK IN THE BAHAMAS TAKES MANY FORMS.

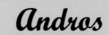

Andros

With a total land mass of 2,300 square miles, Andros is the largest of all the Bahamian islands. It is only twenty miles from New Providence at its nearest point, yet it has its own character and is viewed by some as one of the most fascinating parts of The Bahamas. Andros is made up of a big jigsaw puzzle of islands with hundreds of creeks and rivers, many parts of which have not been explored. There are three large 'rivers' dissecting the land mass at South, Middle and North Bights. Mangrove Cay divides the northern and southern parts of Andros at Middle Bight. Travelling on this large river is like being on the Amazon; there are miles and miles of warm tropical water with an abundance of wildlife on its fringes.

Andros is known for its contrasting ecosystems of pine forests, mangrove swamps, blue holes or hidden lakes, long reefs, agricultural properties and miles of flats. Moreover the western side of Andros is completely undeveloped: apart from Red Bay on the north-west corner of the island, there are no other settlements on the west side of Andros. This makes it a paradise for the wild life explorer who may be fortunate enough to spot flamingos or the six foot long iguanas that the locals claim exist. The eastern shoreline of Andros has many deserted beaches and one coconut grove after another.

The culture and history of Andros is just as interesting as its environment. After the Arawak Indians became extinct, its earliest immigrant settlers were Seminole Indians who crossed the Florida straits in sailing canoes. There is some debate as to when the Seminole Indians came, but their descendants were discovered in a small settlement called Red Bay. The story-telling, myths and superstition that still exist in Andros are believed to result from the Indian influence. The myth of the chickarnie is the most popular; chickarnies are said to be small red-eyed elves who hang from pine trees and cause both good and bad things to happen. The explanation by ornithologists and archeologists, who unearthed fossils, is that the chickarnie was transformed into a legendary creature by people who had seen giant barn owls. The bird, now extinct, was quite large and apparently had a fascinating resemblance to something human. It is also believed that blue holes have monsters living in them, and some of the blue holes are definitely considered off-limits by Androsians.

In Andros, approximately four hundred inland and ocean holes exist. The basic differences between the two are their locations. Ocean holes, as the name indicates, are found in the sea, while the inland holes are completely surrounded by land and at the base are separated from the sea. Ocean holes are also found in the extensive creek system of Andros and differ from inland holes in that there is a very strong current flow. When a tide is flooding or ebbing, at its peak a whirlpool may form at the entrance of the hole. This makes certain ocean holes inpenetrable. Biological factors also vary between inland and ocean holes. The inland holes have an isolated environment that has enabled an assortment of delicate microscopic life to flourish, while in ocean holes a larger variety of species exists. Finally, the inland holes have a fresh water layer at the top which is non-existent in ocean holes.

One very popular and large ocean hole in Andros is called the 'Giant Doughnut'. Half a mile from the shore at Deep Creek, encircled by a magnificent reef environment, the Giant Doughnut awaits the curious observer. This hole is special because it has a wide and deep entrance. Divers who anchor their boats next to the reef must cross staghorn coral to reach the dark blue waters. An opening to the caves in the hole is located at the western part of the entrance and is approximately sixty feet deep. Free diving to the bottom is quite rewarding with rapidly swimming fish darting in all directions.

A reef runs 145 miles along the length of Andros' east coast, limiting approaches to only three breaks: Morgan's Bluff to the north, Staniard Rock Passage and South Bight. The reef is the world's third largest coral reef. There are many spectacular dives up and down the eastern seaboard, because the reef has a dramatic drop more than 6,000 feet into the Tongue of the Ocean. This unusually shaped canyon with only one deep-water entrance has made it a very suitable site for AUTEC. This joint British and US research project is the world's best anti-submarine testing facility.

In the centre of Andros is a very special island called Mangrove Cay. The people have virtually created for themselves a world apart from Andros. They are very

MANGROVE CREEKS ACT AS A NURSERY FOR MANY MARINE CREATURES.

proud of their heritage. You will rarely hear them say, 'I am from Andros'; instead they assert, 'I am from Mangrove Cay.' The intricate creek system found around the island has closed off direct communication to North and South Andros. Boats are the most common mode of transportation and it is no surprise that some of the best boat builders are from Mangrove Cay. Little Harbour is the main town there, from which the weekly mailboat or daily aeroplane can be taken back to Nassau. Andros' most popular summer regatta also takes place there.

Nicholl's Town has the largest population on North Andros, yet it appears to be sparsely inhabited because it is spread over rich farm land where there are cabbages, tomato plants, citrus fruits and even Irish potatoes growing in abundance. It is a friendly community known for its storytellers. In fact it is here that the tale of the chickarnies originated. The English have their fairies, the Welsh their dragons, the Irish their leprechauns and the Androsians have their troublesome, wide-eyed friends of the forest.

Strewn along the shallows on the eastern coast of Lowe Sound are numerous small fishing boats equipped with outboard engines, which are used primarily for lobster and bonefishing. Andros is a heaven for fishermen, especially around Lowe Sound, which is sometimes called 'the bonefishing capital of the world'. There are

POT HOLE FARMING, A UNIQUE METHOD OF FARMING IN THE FAMILY ISLANDS (LITTLE CREEK, ANDROS)

numerous other excellent places where fish can be found in abundance, especially with the aid of a world-famous guide such as Bonefish Charlie.

Morgan's Bluff, located next to Lowe Sound, is named after the celebrated pirate, Sir Henry Morgan. Here the water barges *Mastic Point*, *Black Point*, and the tanker *Minnie Lily* load their cargo of fresh water for the people of New Providence.

The colourful, casual clothing called Androsia began in Fresh Creek. The Androsia factory, producer of bright batik and Island fabrics, is a very important employer in the settlement. The long pieces of dyed fabric are delicately hand-painted and then hung on lines to dry. Next door is the Small Hope Bay Lodge, for the young and not so young who enjoy an adventure above and below the water. Scuba diving is the speciality, but fascinating snorkelling spots are also found in the area.

Andros was named by Columbus 'La Isla del Espirito Santo' or the Island of the Holy Spirit. Maybe that is why there is so much mystery attached to it, yet it is becoming the island of the future. Known as the 'Big Yard', due to its vast landscape and the 'Sleeping Giant', because of its low-key atmosphere, Andros is a relaxed island awakening to the twenty-first century in its own distinctive fashion.

THE COLOURFUL BATIKS FROM ANDROS ARE NOT JUST POPULAR WITH TOURISTS.
MANY BAHAMIANS HAVE ADOPTED THE ANDROSIA FASHION.

Cat Island

Cat Island is not the remotest of islands, but it is one of the least visited. Here, traditions remain strong and the people live off the land as they have done for centuries. The marvellously rich creek systems are home to blue, white, green, great and little herons; the winding branches of seagrape trees drop their ripe purple fruit in calm waters along the many untrodden beaches; and old stone homes and churches, stories passed down over generations, traditions, and rake-'n'-scrape music all add up to something very special. The inhabitants of Cat Island are some of the warmest and most endearing people of The Bahamas.

Situated south-east of Eleuthera, there are 45 miles between Orange Creek in the north and Port Howe at the heel of this boot shaped island.

Supposedly named after a pirate called Arthur Catt, the island is sufficiently large to require two mailboats, yet small enough to ensure that most of the island's residents know each other or are related. Cat Island was once called San Salvador; the older residents still hold land titles passed down from their grandparents which refer to the island by that name. Apparently a cartographic error led to the change in name, but many inhabitants stand firm in their belief that their island was indeed Columbus' landfall.

This is an island of tradition; hidden behind many of the old stone cottages throughout the villages are so-called Dutch ovens. These waist-high rendered domes are still used every day for baking bread. Each oven is shared by several households and they are always built outside to avoid heating up living quarters.

An outsider looking at the soil in Cat Island would be hard pressed to imagine anyone surviving from it. The craggy limestone with its loose rock, pot holes and sparse earth is hardly inviting, yet the Cat Islanders are there to prove its worth.

In fact, farming has always been the mainstay of the economy here. When the large-scale plantation projects of the 1800s failed through over-ambition and the sudden lack of slave labour, the inhabitants developed farming methods more suited to their environment. There are distinct soil types on the island which are good for different crops. For example, the so-called 'white sand' farms are located at Orange Creek in the north. Here, crops such as carrots, beets and potatoes are planted in the loose but productive sandy soil. The richer 'red' soil, found in pockets throughout the island, is good for tomatoes, watermelons and pineapples.

The soil can also be enriched by the use of natural fertilizers, such as the bat guano found in the caves near

Stephenson. It is also improved through the islanders' 'slash and burn' clearing methods; the area to be farmed is painstakingly cleared of bushes and weeds which are burnt, and the ashes are distributed over the land, thereby returning valuable minerals to the soil. The many pot holes are also employed; naturally shaded from the harsh sun and often maintaining a damp loamy soil at the bottom, they make an excellent site for banana plants. The expertise of Cat Island farmers can be seen in every one of the many small settlements that dot the western shores and ridges. They even farmed Little San Salvador, a small island off the west coast.

In the north of the island, Arthur's Town is the main commercial centre with an airstrip and the impressively named Lover's Boulevard Disco and Satellite Lounge. Nearby, the old settlement of Bennett's Harbour is spread around a harbour. With a population of some four hundred, it is one of the largest communities in Cat Island, and the mailboat from Nassau docks here every week. In the adjoining mangrove creeks, eagle rays, sting rays and a variety of marsh birds such as wrens, herons, blackbirds and egrets are plentiful. On the eastern side of Bennett's Harbour are a series of shallow rust coloured ponds. This creek system was expanded during the Second World War as salt pans. Today the area still floods with salt water which evaporates, leaving large deposits of salt which Cat Islanders use in their homes.

Nature has given much to the islanders, but it has also

THE COAST OF CAT ISLAND.

taken much from them. Cat Island has suffered the devastation of several hurricanes in recent history. On the waterfront at the hamlet of Gaitors is a large two-storey home with a basement used as a shelter during hurricanes. Nearby is Poitier Village, where actor Sydney Poitier was born and where a few of his relatives still live.

Towards the south along the island, one encounters the small settlements of Cove, Tea Bay and Knowles Village with its idyllic school right next to the shore. Further south, and most important for the agricultural trade, Smith Bay has a government packing house. Prior to its construction in 1971, farmers sent their produce to Nassau aboard the mailboat to be sold by friends or family members in town. Now, the growers receive regular payments from the packing house, which deals with shipment of the fruits and vegetables.

New Bight, the capital, is situated on a wide bay just above the foot of Cat Island. Visitors generally stay just north of the capital at the Fernandez Bay Village with its beautiful beach. The Armbristers, one of the oldest families of Cat Island, established the beach resort in the late sixties. Many of the most interesting places on the island are close by, the most famous of which is The Hermitage. At the top of the 206-foot Mount Alvernia, at the highest point in The Bahamas, is a monument to one man's faith. The thick walled building is a miniature replica of a Franciscan monastery. John Hawes, known as Father Jerome, built the entire dwelling by himself with native rock. A trained architect and priest, he built the magnificent churches of St Peter's and St Paul's in Long Island. He went on to pursue his faith as a priest in the remoter parts of Australia, but when it came for him to retire, Cat Island was his choice. From The Hermitage, Father Jerome looked out on the clear turquoise waters of the Caribbean to the west and the deep Atlantic blue to the east.

The foot of Cat Island was once the lair of pirates and wreckers. With Columbus Point at its heel and the reef of Devil's Point at its toes, the southern end was treacherous for shipping. The deceptively named Port Howe lies between the two points. It is not a port at all, but a mass of jagged corals where professional wreckers lit fires to deceive unfortunate ships. Arthur Catt also coordinated piratical schemes with his counterparts there. Nowadays, the small settlement is more noted for its lush coconut groves and pineapple fields.

Although the island itself is largely unknown to the outside world, the name Cat Island is well known to all Bahamians through native singer and song writer Tony McKay. His song 'Going to Cat Island' is deservedly popular and on the repertoire of every self-respecting Bahamian band. The lyrics talk of 'rake-'n'-scrape', the traditional entertainment in Cat Island. The sounds of the accordion, a scraped saw, a goatskin drum and a bottle tapped with a nail, join forces in an unmistakably Bahamian sound. Tony McKay calls himself 'The Obeah Man', the name given to Bahamian witch doctors. In Cat Island, superstitions and old stories abound. The obeah man still has a role in island culture, nowhere stronger than in Cat Island. Thankfully, the proud people of Cat Island are keeping their traditions alive in their beautiful home.

LITTLE SAN SALVADOR.

Long
Island

Long is the best way to describe this island geographically. Seventy-six miles long by four miles at its widest part, Long Island stretches south-east from Little Exuma to where the deep Crooked Island passage begins. Diverse is an accurate way to define its population of 3,500. Dotted over its narrow backbone are close to forty different communities with people of different ethnic backgrounds. Self-sufficient well describes the way of life on the island. Long Island is one of the most self-reliant islands, with little help from the outside world. Tourism is not a principal livelihood for the inhabitants here and the main resources are fishing and farming.

Magnificent defines its environment. Here are tall cliffs, peaceful inlet coves, miles of unexploited coral gardens, blooming cactus oases and breeding grounds for sharks and groupers.

In Long Island, there are descendants of many different races who have migrated to The Bahamas. There are white communities from the old Loyalist stock, people with purely negroid features, and most striking of all, Long Islanders with beautiful mid-brown skin and piercing blue or green eyes. It is hardly surprising that the most beautiful women in The Bahamas are said to come from Long Island.

Long Island experienced prosperous seasons of farming corn, cotton and other assorted crops. At the end of the eighteenth century American Loyalists cleared large areas mostly for cotton fields. Stock raising also became popular and continues today, though on a smaller scale.

When slavery was abolished, large plantations could no longer be sustained but, unlike other islands where the land owners left, in Long Island many of the whites stayed. Farming methods changed and the use of natural solution holes for planting began. They called it 'pot hole' farming and its success spread throughout the other islands. Today 'pot hole' farming is still very popular and the islanders will go as far as using dynamite to create this special environment for growing crops.

At the northernmost tip of Long Island is a bold headland named after one of Columbus' ships. Cape Santa Maria has towering white cliffs with a series of caves underneath. On the leeward side of the cape is a stunning white beach. At the tip of the point, a thick barrier reef extends for two miles north of the land. From Cape Santa Maria, Seymour's is the first settlement in Long Island, with many of the homes perched on high ground. Some residents claim that on a clear day Conception Island can be spotted on the horizon.

IN THE WETTER AUTUMN MONTHS, FIELDS OF DAISIES SPRING UP IN THE HOME YARDS
(CLARENCE TOWN, LONG ISLAND).

A few miles south of Seymour's is the smaller settlement of Glinton's. The all-age school for neighbouring communities is located there. Nearby, an old Arawak Indian village was discovered, proof of Arawak occupation on Long Island. One of the oldest buildings in Long Island, at least two hundred years old, is located in the small settlement, Burnt Ground. The rusty red, two-storey structure is covered with vines.

Stella Maris ('Star of the Sea') has been shining good light on the shores of Long Island. The project to develop the resort and its surrounding properties has given jobs to many Long Islanders. The vast range of facilities, including a yacht marina, scuba diving amongst sharks and all manner of land-based sports, has kept this a lively though relaxed resort.

One of the oldest settlements of Long Island, Simms serves the northern section of the island and was named after the first family who settled there during the eighteenth century. The government centre located here consists of the small police station, post office, the telecommunications centre and the magistrate's office. The island's packing house is located in Simms, and once a week the mailboat comes to pick up produce grown and packaged by all the farmers.

Not far south of Simms is Wemyss, where just two families remain in the midst of traces of plantation living. The ruins confirm the hardships the early dwellers must have experienced due to lack of fresh water, poor soil, and primitive fishing methods. Out of frustration, many of these people abandoned the area, returning to the USA and Nassau. The few who remained managed to survive by developing effective methods of reaping the land and harvesting the sea. Here pot hole farming is common, yielding impressive crops. Some of the biggest plantain and bananas grow in natural holes filled with slashed bush watered down by rain thereby keeping the moisture in the soil. Old methods of fishing are also commonly practised, for example using a two pronged spear, called grains, nailed to a staff to catch lobster on moonlit nights.

Salt Pond and Hardings, considered one town, is the next stop going south. Salt Pond was so named for the numerous salt ponds found in the vicinity. The town is known for its fishermen, who catch lobster as their primary source of income. The high price per pound makes it a lucrative profession. The traditional occupations of sponging, sisal farming, salt production, straw work and conching have declined, and in some cases ceased all together. Sailing sloops have been replaced by fast motor boats, and today's fishermen are making good money from the spiny lobster. Consequently life has been modernised in Salt Pond and in some of the other communities. Satellite televisions are becoming common, but families still depend on generators to power them. Like many other southern Family Islands there is in Long Island no public electricity company. Most residents collect rain water in cisterns, and a large water tank was built by the government to supply water to some of the homes.

Most of the land in and around Salt Pond is generation property which was sold or given to the early settlers between 1770 and 1790. The Knowles family is one of the largest; the family's ancestors arrived on the island towards the beginning of the nineteenth century.

Since 1967 during the month of June, Long Islanders have gathered at Salt Pond for their annual regatta; four days of music, dancing, festivities and sailboat races. Sponsored primarily by Nassauvians descended from Long Island, the regatta is above all an opportunity for family reunions and a celebration of the vanishing customs of simple island life. In addition, the efforts of the 'sons and daughters of the soil' who organise this event inject a much needed boost into the local economy by way of prize money, fund raising and the influx of visitors to the island for the duration of the regatta.

While the races are in progess, there is a continuous flow of 'rake 'n' scrape' music, the traditional accordion playing, and the inevitable flow of 'fish stories' related by grizzled, weather-beaten veterans of the sea. Some of the fastest sloops to enter the races were designed and built by Long Islanders like Mr Rupert Knowles of Mangrove Bush who introduced the *Tida Wave,* a frequent winner since 1967 up to the present time.

Between Salt Pond and Clarence Town, twenty miles to the south, there are a dozen or more communities and in the past, there may have been twice as many. The main towns of Grays, Deadman's Cay, Buckleys, Mangrove Bush and Cartwright, all found within a five-mile radius, hold a large part of the population. This is the principal farm land of Long Island where for generations the locals have been growing fruits such as bananas and mangoes and an assortment of vegetables. The central part of Long Island receives more rain and the soil is richer and more productive than in other areas.

By land or sea Clarence Town can be seen from a greater distance than any other community in the Family Islands. The two large churches with their unexpectedly grand towers are an impressive sight. Father Jerome, the famous priest who died in his hermitage on Cat Island, built the two churches on the highest hilltops of Clarence Town. The St Paul's Anglican church was the first one erected, and in later years, when he converted to Catholicism, he built St Peter's Catholic church. From the tower of St Peter's the view of the harbour is spectacular.

Most of the settlements in south Long Island are spread out over a thirty-mile area and almost all of them are situated along the island's main dirt road. From Hard Bargain all the way to Gordon's there are small communities: McKensie, Roses, Taits, Molly Well, Berrys, Cabbage Point, Mortimers and Ford. Roses typifies the nature of these hamlets. There are but two families in the small community; if you are not a Darville then you have to be a Dean. Behind stone walls along the roadside are fields with goats and sheep grazing. Most of the fisherman in south Long Island live in Mortimers and Gordon's and, after a day of fishing, they bring their boats two miles into the creek, which acts as an excellent shelter. In Mortimers there are approximately 120 people, three churches, an assortment of small stores, one school, and one bar. Only one family, the Watsons, live in Gordon's, but at certain times of the year, fishermen from other parts of Long Island camp on the sandy beach. They travel to this remote point to catch the Nassau grouper which congregate to breed. The usually solitary groupers mass in their thousands during certain phases of the moon, just off the shore. Traps set by fishermen are raised and lowered constantly throughout the spawning time. Hungry sharks, which circle the traps as they are hauled in by hand, add to the excitement of this incredible phenomenon.

Life in Long Island is generally tranquil and, according to one of the residents, ideal for raising children as they 'can roam freely without danger'. However, it seems that, upon reaching the age of sixteen most of the young people move away to Nassau or the USA to pursue careers. The people who stay are the builders and developers of Long Island – the diehards. Thanks to them Long Island remains as strong and beautiful as it has for centuries.

San Salvador

Depending on how you look at it, San Salvador is where it all began for the western world or where it all began to end for native Lucayans (meaning island people). They were actually mistakenly named Indians by Christopher Columbus who thought he had reached the East Indies. The Lucayans named the 63-square-mile island Guanahani. It was one of their places of peace and freedom in The Bahamas archipelago.

When the three large ships led by Christopher Columbus arrived on the shores of Guanahani on October 12th, 1492, little did the Lucayans know that their fate would be determined within thirty years. Suddenly their islands were opened up to a group of people with a different background, culture and way of life. The Spanish only saw these gentle and simple people as an easy group to overpower and enslave as workers in the gold mines.

It has been five hundred years since European men discovered the Lucayans and their islands. Yet after so many centuries of change and development, the gentle, simple Lucayan way of life has come back in the hearts of today's San Salvadorans.

San Salvador today belongs to a group of people who work together in unity, honesty and freedom. The exploitation of people as in the days of slavery and the plantation era is in the past. Since then they have been left on their own and learned the soil potential, the native vegetation and the waters better than their predecessors. Everyone is involved in the community. All have concern and feeling for each other. There is hardly ever a face without the island's characteristic friendly and happy smile.

The cross monument at Long Bay is where it is believed Christopher Columbus first stepped ashore. Close by the cross monument is the Mexican monument, signifying the transfer of the Olympic flame from Athens, Greece to the New World for the 1968 Olympics in Mexico City. Only a few miles to the north of the monuments is Cockburn Town (pronounced Ko-burn), the principal town of San Salvador. There the mailboat unloads its goods, and a few paces from the dock are the main telephone station and Commissioner's office. The one and only airstrip and high school on the island are also located in Cockburn Town. Town life centres around the Riding Rock Inn, the softball playing field, and the community disco lounge.

Standing 163 feet above sea-level is the Dixon Hill lighthouse which has been operated manually since it was built in 1887. From the top can be seen the abundance of lakes and creeks which make up the interior of this bean shaped island. The homes of the nearest community,

United Estates, commonly called E.U., can be seen scattered along the creeks where children paddle their home-made rafts between the mangrove passages.

In the past, inhabitants generally travelled by boats and rafts along Pigeon Creek to South Victoria Hill by way of the lakes and creeks throughout the island. Places to the south like Farquharson, Old Place, Trial Farm, Montreal and Allen, that are now practically abandoned, were visited regularly by boat.

It is possible to enter Pigeon Creek through several channels. The shore is lined with tall coconut trees which seem to have been cultivated as shelter for the few stone buildings that house the people of South Victoria Hill. The dock is a small, cement slab. The residents are always eager to greet the few visitors who arrive. James Hanna, whose mother was a bush doctor, will gladly share his knowledge of bush medicine. Samuel Williams is like Hanna a septuagenarian. Minister of the Baptist church, Samuel, like most Bahamians, has that youthful charisma that certainly belies his age. As he stands in old sneakers with his toes popping out, wearing dirty clothes from working in the field, all the passion and devotion this farmer/minister has for the earth is still apparent.

The south-western shore of San Salvador is now completely free of settlements. On the hills overlooking the quaint and attractive bay are the ruins of Watling's Castle, otherwise known as the Sandy Point Estates. The ruins are the remains of a Loyalist cotton plantation. As its name implies, Sandy Point has a wide beach and the periphery of the sand bank sits only yards away from the shore. Just before making landfall, the dark colours of the deep ocean suddenly change to a turquoise-blue.

The reef system just outside French Bay is astonishing. Large stands of coral formations topped with elkorn and staghorn sit in fifty feet of water. Much of the natural environment in San Salvador is the same as it was half a millennium ago. These are only a few of the scenes of the natural world of San Salvador and The Bahamas: half a dozen magnificent frigatebirds, also known as Man-o-War birds, circle gracefully high up in the sky; three iguanas rest motionless in sun-drenched silence, staring at the calm sea from the low sand dune; a humpback whale slaps her pectoral fins, 18-foot wide flukes, on the water's surface; or a rainbow parrotfish snatches quick bites from a piece of grey coral, each bite making an audible crunch.

With the five hundredth anniversary of the discovery of the New World, considered to be the most important historical event since the beginning of time, more attention has been drawn to the discovery island of San Salvador, yet it remains a beautiful example of an unspoiled island that has balanced fame and nature.

A VIEW OF SAN SALVADOR FROM THE MANUALLY OPERATED DIXON HILL LIGHTHOUSE.

Rum Cay

Imagine a far-away island, where glistening beaches are covered with shells, not people, where horses run wild, where fishhawks soar into the sky and spectacular coral gardens are a brief swim from the shore, and where the islanders are delighted to show you around — this is no fantasy, this is Rum Cay. Some of the first Spanish explorers who came here found not only all this beauty, but also a keg of rum washed up on the beach, from which the name Rum Cay was derived. Today, the twenty-square-mile island is often referred to as the 'sleeping beauty of The Bahamas'.

Rum Cay, called Mamana by the native Lucayan Indians and renamed Santa Maria de la Conception by Christopher Columbus, was the second island that Columbus supposedly visited, as it is only 35 miles from San Salvador.

Since Columbus first visited Rum Cay, the island has experienced a series of economic booms and busts. Apart from pirating, the major legal industries that thrived on the island were pineapple, salt and sisal. Today, the majority of the ninety or so residents fish, farm, collect seashells, plait straw and cater to tourists.

Rum Cay's total population resides in Port Nelson, originally called Wellington Bay. In the past there were other communities found all over the island, with names like Port Boyd, Carmichael, Black Rock, Times Cove, The Village and Gin Hill. Although it is overgrown with vegetation, signs of homes can still be seen in these abandoned areas.

The early plantations in Rum Cay produced mostly cotton and some pineapple. To define properties and keep animals fenced in, walls were built by slaves all over the island. These stone walls, called 'margins', can still be seen on the island.

There were two major hurricanes, still remembered by the older generation, in 1908 and 1926. They were responsible for a lot of damage on the island and, although people were already moving off the island, after the 1926 hurricane many more residents left. The existing plantations, and the salt industry which was the most prosperous in The Bahamas at the time, were completely devastated.

Sisal on the other hand survived through the hurricanes. A thick-leafed plant, sisal was used for making rope until the late 1930s when nylon rope replaced it. When sisal growing was finally phased out there were no more major industries left on Rum Cay. Seashells were occasionally collected for making jewellery; and although goats and cattle were raised for meat, the pastures were not kept properly fenced and many of the animals ran wild. Many animals still roam in the blackland coppice. Although it would have been the best area for growing crops, the herbivores kept ravaging the fields. Now islanders go hunting for wild goats, but sometimes a cow is shot. Healthy horses live in a valley on the most remote side of the island.

The older folks of Rum Cay will tell you that life was much better in the past. There were successful industries and people to run them. The 1926 hurricane keeps coming back in their memories. The main history of Rum Cay comes from the days before that vicious storm. Residents still refer to an old man named 'Papa' Clayton Foster who lived to be 106 years old. He '*first* had sense', an expression meaning he could remember as far back as possible in time.

In Rum Cay the diving is one of a kind. One area

SPECTACULAR DIVING OFF RUM CAY.

referred to as the Grand Canyon has gigantic coral walls rising from the ocean floor, from sixty feet down almost all the way to the surface. In certain reefs around the island, scores of highly valued Nassau groupers and other fish congregating around visiting scuba divers can be found.

Conception Island

It is not surprising that Conception Island has been named a land and sea park by The Bahamas National Trust. To the west of it is Southhampton Reef, a fabulous reef system extending like a coral tail and twice as long as the island itself. The virgin reef alone is worth protecting. The island is regularly visited by a number of migratory birds and by the endangered green turtle who comes there to lay her eggs. The removal of eggs is absolutely forbidden.

The bay where the turtles can safely bury their eggs in the sand also provides an excellent anchorage for sailors during prevailing winds and has one of the largest beaches in The Bahamas. Fields of seaoats swaying in the wind, low-lying seagrape trees growing out of sandy soil and an abundance of prickly pear cactus can be found on the elevations surrounding the bay. The fruit of the latter can be eaten, but extreme care must be taken with the spines. Rubbing the fruit back and forth on a hard surface will break the spines off. Then it will be safe to split the fruit open and eat the juicy red contents. Family Islanders occasionally make prickly pear jam from the cactus.

Round the southern point of the bay, approximately half a mile down, is the entrance to the interior creek system of the island. At high tide the surface area of the water in the interior is greater than that of the total land area. Only certain parts of this shallow lake are accessible by boat; nevertheless, the sight of deeper opal-blue water weaving through the white sandy grounds is never to be forgotten.

CONCEPTION ISLAND.

The Crooked Island District

The Crooked Island District comprises three major islands (Crooked, Acklins and Long Cay) covering approximately 260 square miles of dry land which curves around a large area of shallow bank water. The island trio, the adjoining cays and the inland waterways are still undisturbed by modern technology and large scale development and so remain very tranquil.

In the nineteenth century, the district had more people than most of the other Bahamian Islands. Albert Town, on Long Cay, was a principal port of entry for commercial boats and the capital of the district. Three to four thousand people lived on Crooked Island and as many on Acklins. Long Cay then had close to two thousand people. When steam power replaced wind power and the Panama Canal opened, the trans-shipment line was closed and the population diminished rapidly. Today, the twenty-six individuals living on Long Cay have adapted to living in small numbers and surviving off the bounty of the sea.

There are no major settlements in the district, but many small communities live in partial self-sufficiency, following a traditional way of life. The islands have a diverse and rich environment. The undersea life is fabulous, with numerous unexplored areas. Most of the birds that visit The Bahamas and all the others that are established residents, find refuge in these peaceful isles. Waking up with the sun in the morning or watching it set in the evening will reveal wild flamingos playing in the shallows or just flying overhead.

Crooked Island

Crooked Island derives its name from the shape of the land. In the isolated shallows at French Wells, on the creeks and lakes at Turtle Sound, on the roads surrounded by rolling bluffs, on the countless unspoiled beaches and virgin reefs and in the friendly communities from Landrail Point to True Blue, there is an island that twists and turns with rarely a dull moment to be discovered.

With 92 square miles of land area, the island is larger than New Providence, but its population today is less than six hundred all told. In Landrail Point, at the northern point of the island, most of the residents are Seventh Day Adventists; consequently, there is no alcohol or tobacco sold here. The government dock is located here, and the mailboat docks once a week.

Two and a half miles north of Landrail Point is Pittstown. It is believed that an elevated point lying just beyond the Pittstown Landing Hotel was at one time used by pirates as a lookout point. Because residents found cannons there, it was named Gun Bluff. Adjacent to Gun Bluff is a quarry which provided stone for the 112-foot-tall lighthouse on Bird Rock.

Around the point from Bird Rock, the friendly community of Moss Town consists of a collection of small houses scattered along a hillside where yellow elder, the national flower, blooms in the gardens. From the top of the hill, the opal-blue waters of Turtle Sound spread out to the south. The waterway swirls through the mangroves, home to numerous wading birds and hawksbill turtles.

In the past, residents reached Moss Town through the extensive creek system and lakes of Turtle Sound. Generally, these were fishermen who fished in the sound itself or who would leave the waterways to catch conch on the banks called the Bight of Acklins. There are few landing stations within Turtle Sound, and today 'the number one', which connects to Cabbage Hill by a long track road, is the only one used. Visiting sailors are impressed by the large sound with its tall cliffs, cactus blooms and mangrove passages.

Further east is the most populous settlement on the island – Cabbage Hill. The town has three bar rooms, one food store, one guest house, two churches, one auto repair store, a barber shop, and even a beauty salon.

Adjacent to Cabbage Hill is Colonel Hill, the capital of Crooked Island. At the top of the Hill is the Commissioner's residence and a few other homes. From there, the colourful homes in the valley and the large unnamed harbour in the background provide one of The Bahamas' most picturesque views.

Acklins

Acklins has remained unknown to the world, primarily because it lacks the docking facilities and accommodations found in other Family Islands. Although it is among the most southerly of the islands in The Bahamas archipelago, and the sailing is more challenging because of the reefs, those who have explored its rich underwater environment and wildlife will tell you it is simply one of the most beautiful places in the world.

Snuggled right upon Crooked Island, Acklins is only separated from its neighbour by a few miles. A ferry boat makes two journeys a day (8 a.m. and 4 p.m.) from The Ferry on Crooked Island to Lovely Bay in Acklins. In Lovely Bay the centre of town is only a few paces to the east and within one block there is a very small store with only a few items and a local bar

CARRYING WATER FROM THE COMMUNITY WELL
(MOSS TOWN, CROOKED ISLAND).

which also serves as the telephone station. Lovely Bay's homes are set along the shores, shaded by coconut palms and dilli trees.

Interestingly, Acklins' proximity to Crooked Island has not created a mix of people. Apparently, there was traditionally very little communication between the two islands, and, in some cases, between two settlements on the same island. The only group of people who occasionally saw each other were the seafarers; otherwise, the farmers rarely left their home ground. Some of the towns were separated by thirty miles and journeying back and forth took a full day. The only person who would make regular trips on the track roads was the mail messenger.

Because of this semi-isolation some communities adopted different dialects. A good example survives in Salina Point. Located at the southern tip of Acklins and removed from other settlements, there is a variation in word pronunciation there.

Today, unpaved roads run between all the settlements of Acklins so there is active communication, mostly by sturdy trucks. As always, the mailboats faithfully visit this Family Island, and make stops at Spring Point, the capital, and Chesters, a small boat building community on the northern part of the island.

Unlike most other Bahamian Islands, in Acklins communities are found equally on both the windward and

ONLY A HANDFUL OF PEOPLE IN TWO SMALL COMMUNITIES LIVE ON THE ISOLATED NORTHERN COAST OF ACKLINS.

leeward side of the island. On the windward side, which is exposed to the prevailing winds and where ocean swell breaks up on the continuous reefs, there are communities such as Lovely Bay, Chesters, Pinefield and Salina Point. Along the protected leeward coast there are settlements like Snug Corner, Spring Point, Delectable Bay and Binnicle Hill.

Since the middle of the eighteenth century, islanders from Acklins have been cutting the bark from the shrub *Croton cascarilla*. Initially, the bark was used for medicinal purposes and sometimes up to sixty tons of it were exported each year. Today, the bark is still stripped off the shrub and sent via Nassau to Italy where it is used to flavour the popular Campari liquor.

In Delectable Bay, Mr Elkin Roker is one of Acklin's cascarilla merchants. He represents one of many individuals in the district who have industriously collected the bounty of the land and sea. His father collected sponges when the industry was booming, and he continues, at a much smaller level, to send sponges to Nassau. His greatest pride was when he had one of the only large scale aloe vera plantations in The Bahamas. Pronounced 'halawis', the islanders still use the cactus for making medicinal cures to treat aching stomachs. Cutting one of the spike-like leaves, Roker advises the visitor to 'use dis halawis when yer belly hoytes bad or when da sun buynes yer skin.'

The Cays of the District

In this area water is completely different from one side of the cays to the other. To the east, the water is extremely shallow and is divided by a series of long, narrow sand banks. Snorkelling in two to four feet of crystal clear water will show the diver an abundance of juvenile conchs, which should not be collected as there are larger ones in the six to ten foot water between the cays. On the western side, the water is deeper and dotted with a collection of small but fruitful reefs. These are called 'heads' by the locals and, in a space smaller than a garage, thrive a multitude of life forms. For example, exploration of a half dozen heads found half a mile off the Guana Cays will reveal every

FISH CAY, CROOKED ISLAND DISTRICT.

possible species of coral and reef fish. Even a hawksbill turtle may be found snuggled under a coral ledge.

North of the Guana Cays is Fish Cay, where a large population of small iguanas live. At first, it is hard to discern their presence, but looking at the crisscross pattern of trails on the sand underlines their presence. Unlike the iguanas on Allan's Cay in the Exuma Cays, these iguanas are extremely shy.

Long Cay

During the late nineteenth century, the Crooked Island District experienced an economic boom thanks to Long Cay (formerly known as Fortune Island). A major shipping port, Long Cay was a busy island, and Albert Town was one of the most prosperous settlements. There were streets connecting the entire island, with homes, stores, saloons and one large Catholic church (still standing) lining them. Street lights illuminated the roads at night for residents riding in their horse-drawn carriages, and the island even had a railway system.

Today, the 23 or so individuals who live on Long Cay, all fishermen, are quite content with the slow pace and the tranquillity. On the eastern part of the island is a sanctuary for the West Indian flamingo. Approximately three hundred of these magnificent pink birds use the sand spits during the day as resting grounds; the flamingos can also be seen in French Wells, the cut between Crooked Island and Long Cay, which is actually one of the most popular stopping grounds in the district for yachtsmen.

Words and pictures cannot give an adequate picture of the beauty found in the Croooked Island District. Once seen, the image of these beautiful islands is hard to forget.

The Far Southern Islands

Inagua

Far, far away in the southernmost regions of The Bahamas archipelago is Great Inagua, a rugged island where the people, the wildlife and the salt industry thrive in harmony and prosperity. Forty miles long by twenty miles wide, Great Inagua is the third largest of all Bahamian islands; the land of sun, sea and salt. Inagua has a successful blend of industry and wildlife. Tall heaps of salt produced from the large, shallow lakes provide a brilliant backdrop to the graceful flamingos flying by.

Historically, solar salt processing dates back to the 1600s. In those days, ships would stop over in Inagua to load salt destined mostly for Cuba and Hispaniola. Actually, Inagua is only eighty miles from either island and on a clear night, lights on the mountaintop of Haiti can be seen.

Salt was harvested in Inagua on a small scale until 1849 when a company upgraded the production system by using mule-powered rail cars. The salt was kept in a specially built storage building called the Salt House, which still stands today. In the nineteenth century, the salt was used primarily for preserving meats and other perishable food items.

Before the end of the First World War, the population in Inagua was above 5,000 and it was, along with Albert Town in the Crooked Island District, a main port of entry for ships entering the northern part of the Windward Passage. The Hamburger American Line and the Netherlands Steamship Company were the two major shipping companies among those which stopped over in Inagua to take on stevedores, contract workers, salt and supplies.

The unionisation of stevedores and migrant workers stopped the shipping activity in Inagua. The population rapidly diminished, and prosperity on the island only returned in 1936, when the three Erikson brothers from America arrived on the shores of Inagua. The Eriksons' purpose was to establish a large mechanised solar salt evaporation project and the ideal environment found in Inagua enabled them to do it with great success. The only opposition they faced came shortly after they were established when two brothers, George and Willis Duvalier, intentionally moved in on Inagua to oust the Eriksons. The Duvaliers were soon accused of arson and murder and were sent to Nassau where they were tried and hung. The Eriksons returned from their refuge in Cuba and continued salt production in Inagua.

In 1954, the Eriksons sold the business to the Morton Salt Company, which changed the name to Morton

Bahamas Limited identifying it as a Bahamian operation. Improvements were immediately undertaken by Morton Bahamas Ltd (MBL). A dock was constructed to accelerate the shipment of salt, and a large ocean-going vessel, the *Cecil Erikson* was specially built for salt transportation.

The interior of Inagua consists of thousands of acres of very shallow water holding billions of gallons of highly concentrated salt water. It is estimated that for every gallon of this seawater a quarter of a pound of salt can be extracted by evaporation. Such facts point to the potential success of processing salt in Inagua. Moreover, Inagua has plenty of sun and wind, both of which play a crucial role in evaporating the water and drying the salt. There is also a low rainfall. The industry is also successful because of the people. The Inaguans are salt people who for generations have been raking salt. In Matthew Town, there is a feeling of pride amongst the thousand easy-going people who live in a community where the majority survive off the 'white gold'. 'Hospitality Unlimited' is how many people of the one and only settlement of Inagua have been described.

While salt reigns in Inagua, so does its population of West Indian flamingos, the largest colony of this kind in the world (approximately 50,000). In 1950, Robert Porter Allen, at the time the director of research for the National Audubon Society, found the flamingo to be in perilous straits, its numbers and breeding grounds increasingly endangered by man. A visit to Great Inagua heartened him when local islander Sam Nixon led him to a colony of one thousand pink flamingos. A National Park was established for their preservation and Sam and his younger brother James were its first wardens. Today, James continues his life-long watch over the sanctuary,

with the help of a second generation Nixon, the late Sam's own son Henry. Their near fanatic devotion to these gorgeous pink waterfowl is evident as they patrol the park and escort visitors through the reserve, occasionally stopping to chase away wild boars or even hungry locals seeking the forbidden delicacy of flamingo meat.

The flamingos are not the only beneficiaries of the National Park. Scores of birds populate the island: the indigenous Bahama parrot (which is only found here and on the island of Abaco), roseate spoonbills, egrets, herons, and other water birds. The diversity in species of reptiles, plants and animals is also far greater in Inagua than anywhere else in The Bahamas. The rugged landscape and the extensive lake system in the island's interior has discouraged human settlement, leaving the population concentrated in the protected coastal area of Matthew Town. This has kept the greater part of Inagua untouched and even inaccessible to humans.

On the north-western shore of Inagua, the Nixons supervise another camp called Union Creek, a park founded by the Caribbean Conservation Society and the late Sam Nixon. The purpose of the project was to develop a breeding and research ground for sea-turtles. The enclosed three-square-mile area harbours a number of hawksbill and green turtles and is also referred to as Turtle Sound.

The uninhabited Little Inagua, a smaller, less fre-quented wildlife paradise, is a truly wild island. It is separated from the mainland at Northeast Point, a local hangout for fishhawks, by seven miles of open water. The vegetation is very dense, with intermittent breaks where patches of cactus grow, and where wild donkeys have made trails. There are also several lakes frequented by flamingos, and many high cliffs and hills. In the centre of the island, within a square mile area, are enormous circular holes containing open grottoes and pools of the purest rainwater. Within a bed of long grass grow tall indigenous royal palms. Reaching one hundred feet high, these clusters of royal palms are believed to have survived there for centuries.

Inagua is a special island. It has industry, energetic and kind people, an unlimited source of wildlife and a

INDIGENOUS ROYAL PALMS RISE FROM THE FRESHWATER SOLUTION HOLES AT THE CENTRE OF LITTLE INAGUA.

progressive economy. If Morton Bahamas Limited continues to provide for the people of Inagua, the troublesome exodus prevalent on other Family Islands will not occur here.

Mayaguana

Mayaguana is unlike the islands of the Central and Northern Bahamas which are surrounded by extensive shallow seas of the Great and Little Bahama Banks. Instead it shares a distinctive feature with the nearby Inaguas, Samana Cay and Plana Cays. A great 'wall' drops from near the shores to a depth of thousands of feet, and encircles the island. The sheer vertical wall on the western end of the island has towering coralline formations covered with some of the richest and largest variety of marine life in The Bahamas. To the east is Booby Cay where iguanas, flamingos and a score of other birds have found refuge.

AFTER A HEALTHY MEAL, CHILDREN STAND BY THE OUTSIDE KITCHEN.

The land environment is very undeveloped and largely uninhabited, making it one of the most remote and traditional islands of The Bahamas. Fishing and farming are necessary for survival in Mayaguana. Those who fish for a living use small boats from which they collect conch and hook fish for export to Nassau. Families fishing purely for their own needs do so using a line and hook and wade in the shallows along the coast. It is also a good bonefishing ground. After a heavy rainfall there are often many land crabs near the settlements. A lucrative job for young boys is to catch the crabs at night, for sale in Nassau.

Abraham's Bay is the name of both the bay and the town which is situated at its western end. The people of Abraham's Bay are at the mercy of the weather. They cannot irrigate their land, as water is too precious, so they must rely solely on rain. Only crops such as sweet potatoes, pigeon peas and cassava can withstand the dry conditions. Planted in early summer, they are ready to harvest in December. Other crops such as beans and melons must be planted once the heavier rains begin in early fall. Anything that is surplus to local requirement is sold at the Nassau Produce Exchange.

On the west coast is Betsy Bay. The soft, sandy road towards Betsy Bay has tiny hermit crabs that scuttle out of the way leaving tracks that look like those of a giant centipede. Green twenty-foot walls of tall trees and shrubs rise on both sides of the narrow road.

Close by, and of a similar size, is Pirates' Well, which derives its name from the time when pirates would stop by the town for fresh water. Pirates' Well is small and hospitable. The residents make a stop to this lesser known location a worth-while excursion for anyone wishing to acquire a taste for unspoiled Bahamian culture.

In a disused army base near Abraham's Bay, the people have formed a cooperative where all necessary fuels are delivered. Bottles of cooking gas come aboard the *Windward Express* mailboat, but if, as occasionally happens, the boat doesn't come, the residents go without their usual supply of gas, and must resort to using open wood fires.

It is the nature of these people that they would survive with or without a regular supply from Nassau. To an outsider, life here may appear simple and hard. However, many of the inhabitants have a choice. They choose to live spartan lives, but without theft, murder and traffic accidents. There are no bars on the windows and the doors are never locked, but left wide open to welcome in strangers and the sea breeze.

Plana Cays

Approximately 25 miles from Mayaguana is uninhabited East Plana; the approach to this uninhabited island can only be described as wild. A solitary wreck warns of the reef, which in many places breaks the surface with its jagged knives of elkhorn. This small island is home to the shy hutia, a rodent indigenous to the Bahamas. Although the rodent scuttles away timidly, its presence is unmistakable; hutia droppings lie thick on the ground and the foliage has been ravaged by the rodent. Despite its close proximity, neighbouring West Plana bears little resemblance to East Plana. Obviously, the hutias do not live here. This is an island lush with the shining leaves of palmettos and evidence of former habitation – the stone walls of simple houses. Dominating the scene, a magnificent palm gives the final touch to the image of a true desert island.

A FISHHAWK HOVERS ABOVE ITS IMPRESSIVE NEST.

Samana Cay

A relatively obscure island, Samana Cay is hardly mentioned in history books or tourist guides. Also called Attwood's Cay, Samana Cay is part of an uninhabited group of cays, north west of Mayaguana. For decades its greatest claim to fame was that it ranked third, behind Acklins and Crooked Island in the production of the native cascarilla bark. Samana Cay is of particular interest to plant enthusiasts with its rich flora.

The north coast of the island has stretches of shallow reef along a beautiful coast of sandy lagoons. In the south, along another lagoon, are a collection of old ramshackle huts used by the fishermen who come across from Acklins

SAMANA CAY, A CONTENDER FOR THE TITLE OF COLUMBUS' LANDFALL, IS ONE OF THE
LEAST KNOWN BAHAMIAN ISLANDS.

and Mayaguana to fish the bountiful reefs along Samana's shores. Inland there are many surprises: sinnecord trees, wild thyme, cotton and sisal plants.

Samana Cay was pushed into the limelight in November 1986 when Joseph Judge of the *National Geographic* magazine presented his case for Samana Cay as Columbus' true landfall. Even with this international coverage, Samana remains peacefully isolated from the rest of the world.

Hogsty Reef Atoll

Hogsty, four miles of virgin reef in the southern Bahamas, is virtually unknown to mankind. Sitting in the middle of the deep ocean, the coral reef is located almost equidistant from Acklins and Inagua. The practically uninterrupted twenty-mile circumference of vertical wall diving is one of the most striking aspects of the atoll.

Hogsty Reef is one of only two atolls found in the Atlantic. Atolls are formed when the land sinks as a result of sea floor subsidence, leaving the growing reef behind.

The only land remaining, on what a million years ago was a ten-square-mile island, are two tiny cays no more than a hundred yards long. In the summer, South West Cay is a nesting ground for sooty and noddy terns. Hundreds, perhaps a thousand of these birds lay their eggs on the soft sand and allow the hot sun to incubate them. North-West Cay has a small automatic light tower and a single casuarina tree, bent by the continuous trade winds.

The reef is horseshoe-shaped and lies just under the surface of the water, making it a natural graveyard for boats. A large Yugoslavian freighter crashed on the north-western tip of the reef and lies in only eight feet of water. All other wrecks, except for the mailboat *Lady Eagle*, are under water. Some of them may possibly date from the days of the Spanish conquistadors. A few large anchors are the only signs left from this period, as much of the debris has been swept away with the currents and the gold has been salvaged.

Inside the horseshoe is a sandy lagoon where coralline structures are scattered about. Along with the vertical coral walls, these are the homes to probably the most plentiful marine life found in The Bahamas.

(ABOVE) A CURTAIN OF BLACK RAIN DARKENS THE HORIZON. HEAVY DOWNPOURS
OCCUR IN HOT SUMMER MONTHS AND ARE A BLESSING AS THEY SWEEP THE LAND.

(OPPOSITE) SHALLOW SHOALS STAND OUT IN THE CLEAR TURQUOISE WATERS OF THE BAHAMAS.

THE GRUNT, AN ABUNDANT
REEF FISH, IS NAMED FOR
THE SOUND IT MAKES.

GREAT BARRACUDAS
PATROL THE WARM
BAHAMIAN WATERS.

S CUBA DIVING AMONGST THE CORALS.

D RAMATIC CORAL FORMATIONS IN THE
REMOTE WATERS OF HOGSTY REEF.

MIGRATING SOUTH DURING THE WINTER MONTHS, THE ATLANTIC
POPULATION OF HUMPBACK WHALES PASS THROUGH THE BAHAMAS.
THESE GRACEFUL CREATURES CAN REACH A LENGTH OF SIXTY FEET.

THE BROWN PELICAN, JUST ONE OF
THE NUMEROUS AVIAN INHABITANTS
OF THESE ISLANDS.

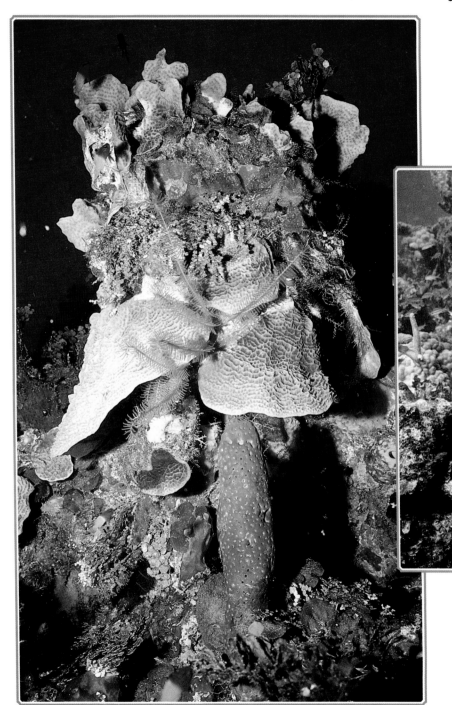

THE DELICATE STRUCTURE OF THE
BRAIN CORAL, JUST ONE OF THE
MANY BEAUTIFUL UNDERWATER
FORMATIONS.

A CLUSTER OF COLOURFUL
CORALS AND SPONGES.

113

A NIGHT CROWNED HERON
WATCHES FOR FISH FROM
A COCONUT TREE.

THE BAHAMA PARROT
IS FOUND IN ABACO
AND INAGUA.

WEST INDIAN FLAMINGOS IN FLIGHT OVER THE CROOKED ISLAND DISTRICT.

POINCIANA BLOOMS ARE
A SPECTACULAR SIGHT
IN SPRING AND SUMMER
ALL OVER THE BAHAMAS.

THE SCARLET POINSETTIA
ADDS A SPLASH OF CRIMSON
TO THE LUSH FLORA.

RIPE PURPLE SEAGRAPES
HANG IN HEAVY CLUSTERS
ALONG BAHAMIAN SHORES.

WOMEN WASHING, CAT ISLAND.

CROOKED ISLAND.

An old lady, Eleuthera.

(Opposite)
Goin' line fishin'.

THE HERMITAGE
ON CAT ISLAND.

A COLONIAL STYLE GOVERNMENT BUILDING IN
ROCK SOUND, ELEUTHERA.

A ROOF WINDOW IN
SPANISH WELLS.

DRESSED FOR CHURCH. THE SUNDAY SERVICE IS A SOCIAL AS WELL AS A RELIGIOUS OCCASION.

As well as spear fishing, the fishermen trap large grouper. Once caught, the load is hauled up manually from a considerable depth.

Nassau grouper, scaled and gutted for market.

A SPINY LOBSTER, OR
'CRAWFISH', SEEKS SHELTER IN
A CORAL CREVICE.

CONCH MEAT IS 'KNOCKED'
OUT OF ITS SHELL AND
PREPARED FOR MARKET.

(OPPOSITE) BONEFISHING IN THE
SHALLOW FLATS OF ANDROS.

INAGUA HAS A SUCCESSFUL BLEND OF INDUSTRY AND WILDLIFE

IGUANAS ARE FOUND IN MANY PARTS OF THE BAHAMAS, BUT THE BIGGEST AND BOLDEST LIVE IN THE EXUMAS.

LAND CRABS ARE CAUGHT AT NIGHT. LURED FROM THEIR HOLES BY FLASHLIGHTS, THE LIVE CRABS ARE KEPT IN PENS. THE TASTY MEAT IS A BAHAMIAN FAVOURITE.

129

THE LEADER OF THE SAXON GROUP.

YOUNG GIRLS ACT OUT THE
POPULAR 'VOLA' DANCE.

JUNKANOO DANCER WITH
LARGE FLOAT PARADE
DOWN BAY STREET.

JUNKANOO IS FOR
CHILDREN AND
ADULTS ALIKE.

THE INTRICATE PAPIER
MÂCHÉ JUNKANOO
COSTUME.

THE BAHAMAS' POLICE MARCHING BAND.

SINGER, SONGWRITER AND ARTIST
TONY MCKAY IS THE MODERN-DAY
VOICE OF BAHAMIAN TRADITION.

THE 'CALYPSONIANS'
PROVIDE THE BEAT AT
THE 'COMPLEAT
ANGLER', BIMINI.

ACTIVE HANDS ON
DECK IN ONE OF THE
ISLANDS' CRUISING
REGATTAS.

(OPPOSITE) SAFE AT
ANCHOR IN THE
BEAUTIFUL BAHAMIAN
WATERS.

THE DOWNWIND LEG.

RACE BOAT *JIFFY* CLOSE-HAULED
DURING ONE OF THE HIGHLY
COMPETITIVE BAHAMIAN REGATTAS.

THE HARBOUR
ISLAND
DISCOVERY
REGATTA.

SPECTATORS IN SPEED BOATS ARE A COMMON SIGHT AT THE FAMILY ISLAND REGATTA.

DOMINOES, A FAVOURITE PASTIME FOR BAHAMIANS ESPECIALLY BETWEEN SAILING REGATTAS.

RESTING BEFORE THE RACES.

Index

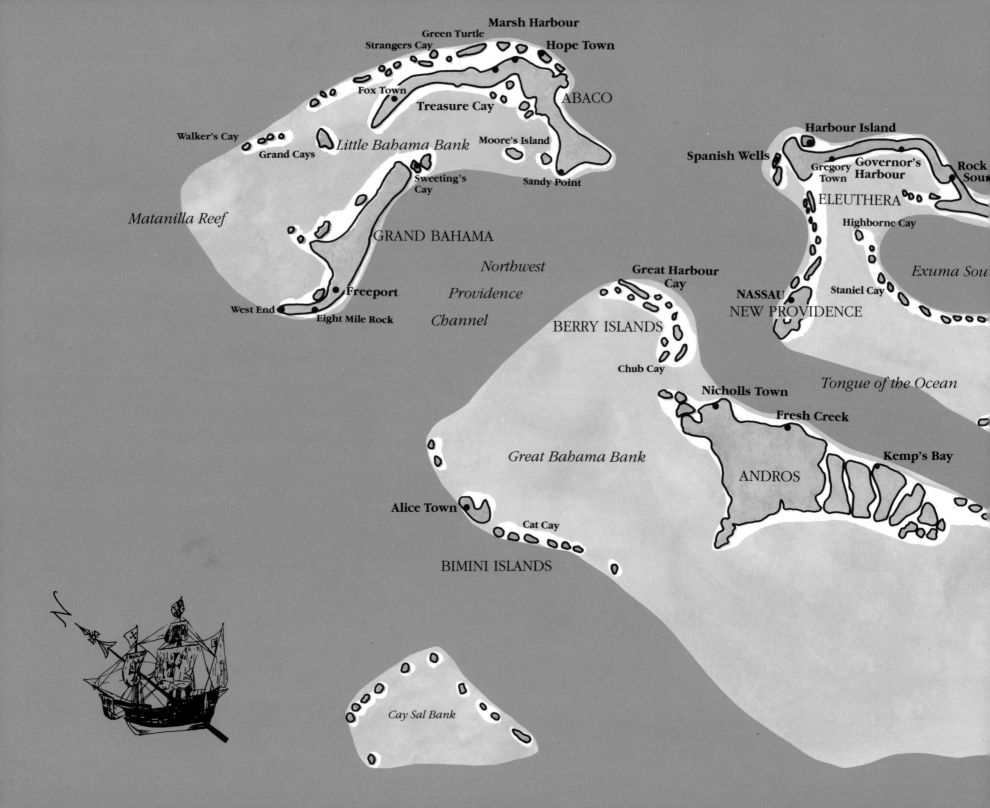

Marsh Harbour

Green Turtle

Strangers Cay

Hope Town

Fox Town

ABACO

Treasure Cay

Walker's Cay

Moore's Island

Little Bahama Bank

Grand Cays

Harbour Island

Spanish Wells

Sweeting's
Cay

Sandy Point

Gregory
Town

Governor's
Harbour

Rock
Sou

Matanilla Reef

ELEUTHERA

GRAND BAHAMA

Highborne Cay

Northwest

Great Harbour
Cay

Exuma Sou

Providence

NASSAU

Staniel Cay

Freeport

Channel

BERRY ISLANDS

NEW PROVIDENCE

West End

Eight Mile Rock

Chub Cay

Tongue of the Ocean

Nicholls Town

Fresh Creek

Great Bahama Bank

Kemp's Bay

ANDROS

Alice Town

Cat Cay

BIMINI ISLANDS

N

Cay Sal Bank